WATCHMAN NEE

Man of Suffering

Bob Laurent

BARBOUR
PUBLISHING, INC.
Uhrichsville, Ohio

Other books in the "Heroes of the Faith" series:

Brother Andrew
Gladys Aylward
William and Catherine Booth
John Bunyan
William Carey
Amy Carmichael
George Washington Carver
Fanny Crosby
Frederick Douglass
Jonathan Edwards
Jim Elliot
Charles Finney
Billy Graham
C. S. Lewis
Eric Liddell

David Livingstone
Martin Luther
D. L. Moody
Samuel Morris
George Müller
John Newton
Florence Nightingale
Mary Slessor
Charles Spurgeon
Hudson Taylor
Corrie ten Boom
Mother Teresa
Sojourner Truth
John Wesley

Published by Barbour Publishing, Inc., P.O. Box 719, Uhrichsville, OH 44683
http://www.barbourbooks.com

Cover illustration © Dick Bobnick.

Member of the
Evangelical Christian
Publishers Association

Printed in the United States of America.

WATCHMAN NEE

I dedicate this book to two of my favorite couples:
Paul and Patti Pauley, whose friendship and love have
meant so much to my wife, Joyce, and me.
Also Ray and Charlotte Cunningham, my "in-laws"
and soulmates, whose passion for foreign missions has
inspired me to finish this project.

prologue

In the summer of 1966, at the same time the Beatles were in their London studios recording "Sergeant Pepper" and Martin Luther King, Jr. was marching through the streets of Chicago, the withered form of a Chinese pastor lay crumpled on the rat-infested floor of his four-and-a-half by nine-and-a-half-foot cell. Located on the backstreets of Shanghai, this vast and hideous onetime British prison had been renamed the First Place of Detention by its most recent landlords, the Red Army of the People's Republic of China. A better name would have been "the Last Place."

After fourteen years of incarceration, the prisoner had made peace with his suffering. Still, last night's beating was perhaps the worst yet. Stirred to a frenzy by Chairman Mao's hostile speech in Peking, the

Communist Revolution exploded on the beleaguered country. Student Red Guards threw down the gates of the ancient Shanghai prison, looking for "counter-revolutionaries" to violently molest. They found Watchman Nee.

And now, his shattered right arm twisted at an impossible angle, the prisoner pulled himself awkwardly from the floor to his cot. He gasped for breath, his failing heart pounding through his chest. Over six feet tall and reasonably healthy at the time of his arrest, he now weighed less than one hundred pounds. A coughing fit seized him, and he accidentally knocked his fractured arm against the wall. Pain shot through his entire right side. His eyes filled with involuntary tears, he raised himself up on his one good arm and through gritted teeth. . .he smiled!

"It could be worse," he thought. "I have not yet suffered to the point of shedding blood," he quoted St. Paul. "And there is still the song. There will always be the song."

As the Shanghai sun lost touch with the decaying city's skyline, a warm, baritone voice that defied its broken instrument made its nightly round of the cell block, easing the despair of the lonely inmates and ending at the battered desk of the hapless guard.

Just a few more miles, beloved
*   And our feet shall ache no more;*
No more sin and no more sorrow;
*   Hush thee, Jesus went before. . .*

As he had done on so many other nights, the brown-shirted guard stole through the shadows, past the rheumy eyes peering in the dark, and crouched by the door closest to the song.

And I hear Him sweetly whispering,
    "Faint not, fear not, still press on;
For it may be over tomorrow;
    The long journey will be done."

After a moment's silence, the jailer whispered, "Pastor Nee, Pastor Nee, are you there?"

"Your questions are always a marvel, Wong Chu-yen. Yes, I am here," came the reply.

"Pastor Nee, your song frightens me. I have not heard it before."

"I have not sung it before. Why does it frighten you?"

"I fear that you are dying."

"No, my young friend. I am much too stubborn to die. And besides, He will not let me come home before you believe."

"But I do believe. I believe you are the best man I've ever known."

"Then you are far from belief, dear Chu-yen. When you have found Christ, you will know that I am the *worst* man that *I* have ever known."

"This talk frightens me more than your death. My poor wife begs me to ignore you. If I follow your Christ, I will end up on the wrong side of this door, and she will be all alone."

"Without Christ, she is alone now."

"Pastor, your words are like hammers on my heart. What must I do to be saved?"

"My beloved Wong, your questions are always a marvel!" Lifting his cadaverous yet radiant face to the ceiling, Watchman Nee softly sang,

"Can you hear Him sweetly whispering?

Your journey has just begun. . ."

Just as Samson killed more of the enemy at his death than he had in his life, so Watchman Nee touched more lives for Christ from the obscurity of his prison cell than he ever had as a free man. His imprisonment for the crime of being a Christian caught the imagination of Western Christendom. So while his Communist captors ordered that his mail be censored and that he not be allowed to mention even the name of God in his correspondence, untold thousands of books containing his sermons and writings were appearing all over England and the United States. By the time his fifteen-year sentence was up and the authorities had increased it by another five to seven years because he would not deny his faith, "Watchman Nee" had become a household name in Christian homes everywhere.

His quiet defiance and seemingly hopeless predicament helped to fuel the fires of the remarkable Jesus Movement that swept from coast to coast in the late 1960s and early 1970s. Mostly unknown to the humble pastor, his name became a touchstone for American believers who were distressed about their brothers and sisters in Christ languishing in Chinese prisons.

Both his cause and his person became legendary to those Christians trying not to take their freedom for granted. Rumors spread that his captors had blinded him for leading his prison guards to faith in Christ. But more of his sermons were published after this. Then it was whispered that the Communists cut out his tongue—but still more of his books appeared. Finally, it was said, they cut off his hands—only to find even more of his writings turning up in the hands of those outside the Shanghai prison. Though some of the stories were exaggerated, they showed the deep concern of fellow Christians over the very real persecution of Watchman Nee.

His captivity made him larger than life, and to this day, no Chinese Christian has had more impact on the lives of believers seeking to remain faithful in the United States. What is the true story of Watchman Nee? You are about to discover it, and as you do, may your faith in Christ grow even stronger.

one

Once, after being viciously criticized by envious colleagues, Watchman Nee was asked by sympathetic friends why he never defended himself. The handsome, young teacher with the perpetual smile replied, "Brothers, if people trust us, there is no need to explain; if people do not trust us, there is no use in explaining." In a country known for its wise men and scholars, Watchman Nee was, perhaps, the wisest of all.

But his wisdom came from a very unusual source for a religious man in China: the Christian Bible. In a land dominated by the superstitions of Buddhism and the ethical teachings of Confucius, Weng-hsiu Nee's son took a resolute stand for Jesus Christ.

Calvin Chao, the exceptional Chinese pastor, said that it takes a "third-generation believer" to communicate with the depth and insight of the great Christian writers down through the ages. Watchman Nee was a third-generation Christian, a fact that is all the more remarkable because, although he wasn't born until the twentieth century, he was one of China's very first "third-generation believers." The reason for this is as interesting as it is tragic.

On the last day of his physical life on earth, Jesus told His followers to go into all the world and preach the gospel, making disciples wherever they went. Apparently those who were heading west heard Him better. They saturated the Mediterranean region with the Good News of Christ within fifty years of Pentecost. Europe was blanketed with the gospel by the start of the third century. But there it stalled for more than one thousand years.

If the early Church had obeyed Jesus and made a right-hand turn at Antioch of Syria (and not only a left toward Rome), surely the history of present-day Communist China would have to be rewritten. If some of the first apostles had preached in the streets of Peking with the same evangelistic fervor they showed throughout the Roman Empire, perhaps today China would be known as a Christian nation. But by the time the Franciscan monks arrived in the thirteenth century with their Western brand of Christianity, the Chinese people were deeply enmeshed in superstition and legalism.

It is tragic that for eighteen hundred years after Jesus died for the sins of the world, the most populated country in the world never really heard the

Good News. Then in 1839, at about the time Watchman Nee's grandfather was born, England declared war on China. After the three-year Opium War, China was defeated and forced to open diplomatic relations with the West. Along with merchant ships delivering opium and seeking silk from the coastal cities of the Far East came zealous Protestant missionaries from America and Great Britain.

The Congregationalists of the American Board chose the seaport of Foochow, an ancient city on the southeastern edge of China. There, in 1853, they started their first missionary school and taught the children about God's great love. A fourteen-year-old boy named Nee U-cheng believed the message and asked Jesus Christ into his heart that summer. When he was later baptized in the nearby Min River, the Nee family's centuries-old enslavement to pagan religion was broken.

U-cheng had a gift for evangelism, which the American missionaries encouraged him to develop. One can only imagine the experiences he and his missionary school friends had when they took to the streets of Foochow to preach the gospel. He was the first Chinese evangelist the city of half a million non-Christians had ever seen. A highly effective preacher, Nee U-cheng was also the first ordained pastor in that part of the world.

When U-cheng was old enough to marry, he had a dilemma. There were few local Christian girls (and none in whom he was interested!), and it was a social taboo to marry someone from outside your province. But U-cheng trusted Christ, and before long a marriage was arranged with a young Christian woman from Kwangtung, almost five hundred miles away. His choice of this feisty Cantonese girl was one he never regretted.

U-cheng and his wife were blessed with nine sons. The fourth son, Nee Weng-shiu, was born in 1877. As a pastor's son, he was educated in Western-style Christian schools and eventually studied at the American Methodist College in Foochow. Weng-shiu was one of the brightest students in his class and was awarded the post of state customs officer.

In 1880, a little girl named Huo-ping was born. Her name means "peace," but for many years she was the least "peaceful" person she knew. The last child of a large peasant family that lived in constant fear of evil spirits, Huo-ping escaped the common fate of female babies last born into poor homes. Instead of being drowned or buried alive by her father, she was sold to a family who intended to make her a slave girl.

God intervened, however, through a wealthy merchant named Lin, who adopted her as his own. After his conversion to Christianity, Mr. Lin saw to it that his new daughter, now called Peace Lin, received a Christian education. She became one of the keenest students in her school. In fact, she was so capable that at the age of sixteen, she was accepted into a program that would eventually take her to a medical school in the United States. But first she had to attend the Chinese Western Girls' School in Shanghai to refine her English skills.

Christian in name only, the school was not good for the young Peace Lin's faith. Daily her worldly ambitions grew as she focused on her appearance as much as her studies. Later in life, she was to write of those years: "I learned there much of the pride of life and some of the sins of the flesh."[1] Then she met the extraordinary Dora Yu.

Dora Yu was not much older than Peace Lin when she came to the Shanghai school as a guest speaker. She told a story that burned into the student's heart. A few years earlier, Dora had done so well in her studies that she was accepted by a medical school in England. She was sent off with great fanfare by her family and friends on a journey she would never complete.

Like Jonah and Paul before her, Dora Yu clearly heard the Lord's voice above the waves while aboard ship. Just past the Suez Canal, He instructed her to give up her career and return to her homeland to preach the gospel of Jesus Christ. Now she stood in the school chapel, passionately testifying to her love for God and challenging the students to commit their lives to Him.

Peace Lin was deeply moved by the penetrating words and humble lifestyle of the visiting preacher, but before she could make a decision about what to do with her life, the choice was made for her. In fact,

Dora Yu's message would wait more than twenty years to have its full impact. For at the age of eighteen, Peace Lin received a letter from her mother stating that an October marriage had been arranged for her with the son of a pastor's widow, a certain Nee Weng-shiu of Foochow.

"Marriage! How I hated that word!" she later said. But spirited or not, Peace Lin would not be the first girl in her province to violate the ancient custom of arranged marriage. Just a few months before the dawn of the twentieth century, the gentle and quiet Nee Weng-shiu married the strong-willed and driven Peace Lin.

About that time, the Boxer Rebellion broke out in Northern China. Had the antiforeign madness spread to the southern provinces, it is likely that both of Watchman's parents would have died along with the hundreds of Chinese Christians murdered in the north.

Instead, they set up house in the little coastal town of Swatow and began their family. After the birth of their first two children (both girls), Peace Lin was beside herself with anxiety and depression. Years later, Watchman Nee himself described the situation:

"According to Chinese custom, males are preferred over females. When my mother gave birth to two girls, people said she would probably be like my aunt, bearing half a dozen girls first. Though at that time my mother was not clearly saved, she knew how to pray. So she spoke to the Lord, saying, 'If I have a boy, I will present him to You.' "[2]

Just as God heard biblical Hannah's desperate prayer for a son, He now heard Peace Lin. On November 4, 1903, Nee Weng-shiu cried out for joy, "It's a boy!" as little Henry Nee was born. The Nees eventually added four more boys and two more girls to their family.

two

"George," said Henry to his younger brother. "I must talk with you. I will explode if I try to keep this inside any longer."

"What's the matter, my brother? You do not seem yourself today."

"That's what I have to tell you, George. I'm *not* myself today. In fact, I don't think I'll ever be myself again." The seventeen-year-old boy told his brother a remarkable story about how Dora Yu, the passionate evangelist, had reentered their mother's life by returning to their city to preach special meetings at the local Methodist auditorium.

By 1920, Peace Nee had drifted far from her Christian upbringing. She'd never forgotten her early poverty or how her arranged marriage had diverted her promising professional career. She became obsessed with political ambition and her social connections.

She later confessed that "from contact with unbelieving revolutionaries, I became almost an unbeliever myself."[1]

But she had not forgotten the ringing testimony of Dora Yu, the woman who had abandoned a lucrative career as a doctor to preach the simple gospel of Christ. And now, Dora Yu's prophetic words cut through the layers of unbelief surrounding Peace Nee after years of self-serving pursuits.

"George, when I saw mother two nights ago, I knew that she had changed," said Henry. "There was an expression on her face I have never seen before. It looked like fear and peace together."

"Mother is afraid of nothing," replied George.

"The fear, I think, was from having been wrong, and the peace was because she has decided to make things right."

"What did she tell you, Shu-tsu?"

"She told me," Henry paused, "that she is a Christian."

"Mother has always been a Christian," came the quick response.

"No, little brother," said Henry. "She said that she has been a lotus plant with no blossoms. But after hearing Dora Yu preach four nights in a row, she could not eat or sleep. Then on Wednesday, she was playing cards as usual with her friends when something broke inside her. She told me, 'I sat there playing as one already dead. Finally, I could take it no longer, and I shouted out to my friends, "I am a Christian!" I shall not play the game again.' "[2]

Henry looked at the picture of his parents on the table near his bed and continued, "And then do you know what she did, George? Mother came home and asked me to forgive her! She threw her arms around me and cried, 'Please forgive me! I confess to beating you unjustly and in anger.' "

"What did you say?" asked George, his eyes growing wider by the moment.

"My exact words were, 'Yes, you did, honorable Mother, and I hated you for it.' Then I turned and left the house."

"Shu-tsu, how could you?" the younger brother scolded.

"Because I was a fool, little brother. But my words punished me all night. I lay in bed thinking that if the power of Christ could move Mother to lose face so badly that she would humble herself to me, then Christianity must be more than another empty religion. George, I went to Dora Yu's meeting yesterday to find out for myself what was going on."

Fifteen years later, Henry Nee told what happened at that meeting:

> *For the first time in my life, I saw myself
> as a sinner, and I also saw the Savior. I saw
> the Lord's hands nailed to the Cross,
> stretching forth His arms to welcome me,
> saying, "I am here waiting to receive you."*

> *Overwhelmed by such love, I could not pos-*
> *sibly reject it. Previously, I had laughed at*
> *those who believed in the Lord, but that*
> *evening I could not laugh. Instead, I wept*
> *and confessed my sins. I prayed for the first*
> *time and had my first experience of joy and*
> *peace.*[3]

That night, Henry knew that God was asking for everything, not a cheap commitment that would ease his conscience for a few weeks. He understood immediately that this was an all-or-nothing decision. "For most people," he said, "the problem at the time of salvation is how to be delivered from sin. But for me, being saved from sin and my life career were linked together. If I were to accept Jesus as Savior, I would simultaneously accept Him as Lord. He would deliver me not only from sin but also from the world."[4]

The apostle Paul was never the same after his vision of Christ on the Damascus road. When explaining his call to preach the gospel, Paul wrote: "For Christ's love compels us" (2 Corinthians 5:14). After Henry Nee's vision of Jesus on the cross, his commitment to preach Christ was no less certain than Paul's and probably no less surprising to his friends. When Paul's associates could hardly fathom that he was the same man who had earlier persecuted the believers, he answered their doubts with, "From now on we regard no one from a worldly point of view. . . if anyone is in

Christ, he is a new creation; the old has gone, the new has come!" (2 Corinthians 5:16,17).

It is customary for the Chinese to choose a new name at a turning point in their lives. When he committed his life to Christ after his family's return to Foochow, young Henry Nee changed his name to Nee To-sheng, or in English, Watchman Nee. Just as Hannah's son, Samuel, warned his countrymen of God's judgment while reminding them of His great love, so Watchman Nee was called to "stand in the gap" for his beloved China.

His friends saw an abrupt change in him also. At Trinity College he stopped cheating on exams, violating the school rules, and leading his friends in open ridicule of Christian classmates. In fact, after a lengthy bout with a guilty conscience, he screwed up his courage and approached the principal's office one day.

He knew that the penalty for cheating was prompt expulsion, but the love of Christ was compelling him to confess. Besides, upon conversion, he abandoned all his previous career goals of becoming wealthy and well positioned. In fact, on the very evening he was saved, he chose for his lifetime career the one profession he had once labeled "the most despised and base of all occupations": preaching.[5]

"One cannot both preach and cheat," he thought. That day, the school principal heard an interesting confession between classes. Apparently he was impressed by the student's integrity and the strength of his

Christian convictions, for there were no students expelled from Trinity.

The die was cast. Watchman Nee set his hand to the plow and did not look back. As a seventeen-year-old boy, he vowed, "I will give Christ all of my life, my loyalty, and my love"—and he never went back on his word.

three

In the spring of 1920, the same season of Watchman Nee's conversion to Christianity, another young Chinese (only ten years older than Watchman) was completing his conversion to the gospel of Karl Marx. Mao Tse-tung, born into a peasant family, had participated a few years earlier in the People's Revolution. He'd done his part to sweep away the Imperial Dynasty that had controlled China for centuries.

And now, as Mao sought out a mentor who could teach him Marxist ideology, the adolescent Watchman was looking for a guide who would train him in godliness. Mao Tse-tung searched for a political connection that would help prepare him to ascend one day to the leadership of China's Communist Party. Watchman Nee prayed for God to send him a mature believer who would teach him the deep truths of God's Word.

Mao found the militant atheist Chen Tu-hsiu, who would later direct the persecution of Christians as secretary general of the Communist Party. Together they would rule China with a ruthless hand. Watchman found Anglican missionary Margaret Barber, and together they laid the foundation for the Christian church in China.

While Mao Tse-tung was studying Marx, Hegel, and Nietzsche, Watchman Nee was poring over John Bunyan, Andrew Murray, and the Bible. Two young minds set on different tracks—with the destiny of China at stake.

After His baptism, the Lord Jesus was driven by the Spirit into the wilderness for forty days and nights of temptation. After his conversion, Paul was led into the Arabian desert for three years of study and reflection. After Watchman Nee came to Christ, he was directed by God to Margaret Barber's mission at White Teeth Rock, just outside Foochow. There he encountered one of the most unforgettable characters he would ever meet, a woman who would teach him lessons for a lifetime of ministry.

Margaret Barber never did anything the easy way. As a vibrant, single woman in her twenties, she traveled alone from England to China in 1899. Laboring for Christ in obscurity, she threw herself into the work at the girls' middle school in Foochow. When she finally took a furlough after ten years, envious coworkers took the opportunity to slander her good name to her superior. He believed the fabricated charges and recalled her from the mission field.

By coming forward with the truth, she could easily have vindicated herself and humiliated her accusers. But Margaret was prepared for betrayal. In fact, she had asked the Lord to teach her the "lesson of the cross." As the "sheep before his shearers is dumb," so Margaret would not defend herself. Even after the truth was later discovered and her bishop offered full restitution, she would not lay down the cross and accept reinstatement. Instead, stripped of all financial support, she returned to China with a new awareness: she had nothing to fear from men or their institutions. She was a person of the cross, crucified with Christ and therefore disinterested in mere mortal opposition.

It seemed impossible to stop her faith. Old enough to be his mother, Miss Barber inspired Watchman with her radical devotion to the cross and her unflagging passion for God's Word. Isaiah 44:3 says, "I will pour out my water on the one who is thirsty." Watchman was thirsty, and God used Margaret Barber's teaching to pour out His water.

For her part, Margaret had prayed the year before that God would raise up young men and women of China to reach their country for Christ. *Could To-sheng be an answer to my prayer?* she wondered. If so, she would sharpen him as iron sharpens iron.

"Stay broken," she would often say to him. "Don't believe all the good things people say about you. You must stay broken. His Word says that if your ways are pleasing to the Lord, He will make your enemies to be at peace with you. He is most pleased with your brokenness. Remember the cross, To-sheng. You must stay broken."

And Miss Barber made sure he learned that lesson well. After Watchman joined her in ministry, she purposely put him under the charge of a supervisor who drove him to distraction. Watchman's temper flared up every time he disagreed with this man, who was a few years older but not nearly as gifted as he. Following each controversy, Watchman would find Margaret and heatedly state his grievances.

"He's wrong again!" To-sheng would claim. "He never does anything the way I know it should be done. You must speak to him and correct him."

Predictably, Margaret would firmly reply, "The Scriptures say the younger should obey the elder. You have much to learn," she said, closing the matter. Time and again, Watchman would walk away angry with her, the Scriptures, and life in general. But slowly the lesson began to take hold. Later he would write,

After a dispute, I would go to Sister Barber hoping that she would vindicate me. But I would weep again after she said, "Whether that coworker is wrong or not is another matter. While you are accusing your brother before me, are you like one who is bearing the cross? Are you like a lamb?"

*When she questioned me in this way, I felt
very ashamed and I could never forget it. . . .
In that year and a half, I learned to obey an
elder coworker and I came to realize what it
is to bear the cross.[1]*

Like Margaret Barber before him, Watchman
eventually became a "person of the cross" and
refused to defend himself when falsely accused.
Once, while single and living in Shanghai, he was
visited for a time by his mother, Peace Nee. Rumors
began to spread throughout the province that young
Pastor Nee was living in sin with a woman. But he
did nothing to dispel the vicious lie. On the contrary,
when begged by his friends to reveal the truth, he
simply said, "The lower we put something, the safer
it is. It is safest to put a cup on the floor." That was
Watchman's way of saying that the more a Christian
is humbled, the safer it is for him. In fact, the safest
place this side of Heaven is the cross.

Watchman learned other important lessons from
Margaret that were to play key roles in his ministry. For
example, she couldn't find a scriptural basis for
denominationalism, the unfortunate phenomenon of
believers separating into various "brands" of Christianity. Watchman deplored the church being divided
and even came to believe that denominationalism was
condemned by Scripture, according to 1 Corinthians
1:10-13. He was later criticized for his conviction that
there should be only one church in each locale.

Margaret Barber lived daily with the expectation that Christ might return any moment. One day, when she and her favorite student were out walking and approached a street corner, she exclaimed, "Perhaps as we turn the corner we will meet Him!" Under her tutelage, Watchman thrilled to the doctrine of Christ's imminent return and kept it at the forefront of his preaching.

Margaret Barber's friendship and Hudson Taylor's biography had the most influence on Watchman's relationship to money. He knew of Taylor's commitment to tell God alone of his financial needs, and he saw Miss Barber live out that very principle. Because she chose to accept no support from any missionary organization and to live by faith only, Margaret moved from one financial crisis to another. But she refused to panic and ask any human to bail her out. It was God who "owned the cattle on a thousand hills" and He who said that He would supply all her needs "according to His riches in Christ Jesus."

Watchman was so impressed by the unusual ways that God consistently would get the money to her, and often just in time, that he decided he would live by faith also in this matter. It was not an easy decision to make for a young man who had ample resources available to him for the asking. But it was another "Barberism" he would not regret taking on.

Once, as a novice preacher, Watchman decided to trust God completely for his needs. He had read three Scripture passages that he could not get out of his mind: the story of God directing the ravens to feed Elijah by the brook Cherith, the story of God filling the large jars borrowed by the widow of Zarephath with the little oil left in her tiny jar, and Jesus' promise in Luke 6:38 that if we give, it will be given back to us, full and overflowing. Now it was time to take God at His Word.

Watchman was invited to preach in a city far to the north in his province. He had only fifteen dollars, about a third of what he needed for the trip. On the morning of his departure, he was praying for God's provision when he felt impressed to give five dollars of his meager funds to a coworker. "But, Lord," he argued, "I must leave to do your work tonight, and I'll never find a boat to take me for less than forty dollars." With tears in his eyes, though, he found his colleague and surprised him with the gift of five dollars, saying, "Don't ask me why; you will know later."

He set out to catch his boat, not even knowing how to pray except to say, "Lord, You know what You're doing." When he got to the wharf, a boatman approached him, saying, "I have one space left at the stern, and I don't care how much you pay me. Let's say seven dollars and you provide your own food." The tears returned to the young preacher's eyes.

As the meetings drew to an end, he realized he had the same problem again. He began praying on Saturday for the money for his Monday departure. On Sunday evening, a certain Mr. Philips invited him to dinner and after the meal said, "Mr. Nee, you have done so much for our church in these past days that we would like to pay for your travel expenses both ways."

Watchman's heart leaped at the offer, but he heard his voice saying, "No, my friend. That is very generous of you, but someone has already accepted this responsibility." Somewhat put off, the gentleman offered him a devotional book instead, and they parted company for the evening. That night, Watchman's thoughts were confused.

"Lord, was that You who had me turn down Mr. Philips's gift? Was he the one You wanted to provide for me? Do I have to ask a friend now to loan me the money? Lord, how am I going to get home?!"

The next morning, with just a few dollars in his pocket, he walked to the boat, wondering if he'd made a mistake yet excited to see how God was going to provide again. Even before he reached the wharf this time, someone ran up to him with a letter that read:

> *Dear Mr. Nee,*
> *Though someone else has assumed the responsibility for your traveling expenses, I feel that I should have a share in your work here. Please be good enough to accept this small sum for this purpose.*
>
> *Rev. Philips*

What could Watchman do? Pastor Philips had

purposely not come so that he could not be turned down again. Watchman boarded the boat more certain than ever of God's provision, and he would preach this truth all his life:

"As God sent the ravens to feed Elijah, he will do the same for you today," he taught with conviction. "If you trust in Him, the less money you have in your hand, the more He will give you," he preached from experience. "God's supply arrives just when you have spent your last dollar," his listeners often heard him say.

When Watchman arrived home in Foochow, one of the first people he encountered was the grateful wife of his coworker, who tearfully told him, "On Friday, we prayed all day because we had no money. Afterwards, my husband felt that he should go for a walk, and then he met you, and you gave him five dollars. The five dollars lasted us through five days."

Softly weeping, she continued, "If you hadn't given us the money on that day, we would have suffered hunger. It doesn't matter that we suffer, but what about God's promise to provide for us?"[2] Watchman was overjoyed by her words and firmly learned the truth that if you give, it will be given to you.

He learned many valuable lessons in the year and a half he was mentored by Margaret Barber. But it was always the "lesson of the cross" he was most grateful for. When Watchman later discipled the young men and women who came to him for mentoring, one could almost hear Miss Barber's voice in his clear teaching:

> *If you cannot stand the trials of the cross, you cannot become a useful instrument. It is only the spirit of the lamb that God takes delight in: the gentleness, the humility, and the peace. Your ambition and ability are useless in the sight of God. I have been down this path; it is not a question of right or wrong; it is a question of whether or not one is like the bearer of the cross.* [2]

It was from Margaret Barber that Watchman took his lifelong motto:

"I WANT NOTHING FOR MYSELF; I WANT EVERYTHING FOR THE LORD."

four

When he wasn't at White Teeth Rock learning from Miss Barber, Watchman was finishing his courses at Trinity College in Foochow and evangelizing everyone he knew. Keeping his vow to read through the entire New Testament at least once a week, he was sarcastically nicknamed "Bible Depot" by his peers. Still, nothing could keep him from witnessing to all of his classmates. "Here comes 'The Preacher,'" they would say at his approach, all the while making snide remarks behind his back. And after almost a year of sharing his faith, not a single person had prayed to receive Christ.

He was beyond discouragement when a coworker at the White Teeth Rock mission told him point-blank: "You are unable to lead people to the Lord because there is something between God and you. It may be some hidden sins not yet completely dealt with or something for which you are indebted to someone."[1]

Watchman was struck hard by these honest words, and he immediately took them to heart. After making a list of every person he could possibly have offended, he went to each of them, confessing his wrongdoing and humbly asking their forgiveness. At the same time, he entered the names of seventy schoolmates into his notebook and systematically began to pray for them individually every day. Within months, all but one of them was born again!

These were exciting days when faith was fresh, ideals were lofty, and the word "impossible" was not in Watchman's vocabulary. With his newly converted friends, wonderfully named Faithful Luke, Simon Meek, and Wilson Wang, he began holding student-led prayer meetings in Trinity's chapel. Before long, the room couldn't hold them and their enthusiasm spilled into the streets of Foochow.

The young men found an attention-getting gong and banged it with abandon in the marketplace. As the crowd gathered, the boys sang joyfully and preached the Good News of Jesus Christ. Then they passed out brochures telling the plan of salvation as they carried large posters to their next preaching location. Foreshadowing the "Jesus T-shirts" that would one day become popular among young American evangelicals, Watchman and his friends created their own unique witnessing wardrobe. They purchased plain white shirts and emblazoned bold Christian messages on them using festive red letters. Soon there were high school students all over the city wearing their "gospel shirts" announcing, "JESUS CHRIST IS A LIVING SAVIOR" and "GOD LOVED THE WORLD OF SINNERS." Something remarkable was happening in Foochow, and the townspeople were beginning to talk about it. God was moving in power among the area's young intellectuals, and the citizens were taking notice.

In the meantime, Watchman was being inspired by his mother's growing faith. Peace Nee was becoming as active in Christian witnessing as she had been in the political arena. Her fiery personality and love for the Bible put her much in demand as an inspirational speaker throughout the province.

One night, after finishing a twenty-day series of meetings at the local YWCA, she was invited to stay on and regain her strength. But from deep within her spirit came a warning that she needed to return home. As she walked that very evening with her husband by the riverfront outside their house, she turned to him and said, "It is so dry tonight; I fear there may be a fire."[2]

Sure enough, in the middle hours of the night, they were awakened by the cries of their neighbors. They stumbled out to the sight of their entire block to the north caught up in a raging street fire. As Watchman's parents knelt to pray with the inferno bearing down on them, Peace Nee was so impressed by the Spirit that their home would be spared that she decided not even to awaken their younger children.

The God who answers prayer responded immediately as the wind miraculously shifted direction, stopping the fire just three houses from their doorstep.

Barely a week later, their faith was more severely tested—again by fire. This time, a stronger wind drove the flames toward them, and the situation looked hopeless. Just as they were about to wake up the children and flee to safety, a very clear thought came to Watchman's mother. "Why don't you pray?" God seemed to be asking her.

She knelt in the midst of the crisis and cried out, "O God, in this quarter of Foochow my family is the only one that believes in You. Give me some answers to these unbelievers so that they cannot say, 'Where is your God now?' "[3]

Again the response was instantaneous. Not only did the wind change to their advantage, but the rain began to fall just as the city's fire brigade appeared from nowhere to use Watchman's home as the base for their firefighting efforts. After two major fires within a week, only five homes remained untouched on the riverside. Watchman and his neighbors were deeply moved by the power of his mother's prayers.

About this time in his life, Watchman fell in love with God's Word. After his conversion, he threw himself into a profound study of the Bible that few historical heroes of the Christian faith could match. From the age of eighteen on, he consistently employed at least twenty different forms of Bible study, from a general study of all the books of the Bible for an overall view, to the intense study of a particular book to probe its depths; from doing word studies in the original Greek and Hebrew languages, to mining the riches of all the Bible's prophecies; from biographical studies of all the characters of the Bible, to a systematic study of all of its doctrines.

He used several different Bibles for specific types of study. One Bible he saved for writing copious notes in the margins as he grew in knowledge of its contents. Another he purposely kept note-free so that he could receive fresh insight every time he took it up. It was not long before Watchman Nee became known as a young man consumed by God's Word. This one characteristic was to set him apart from less-devoted scholars and preachers for the rest of his life.

Of the reading of spiritual books, there was no end in Watchman's routine. He made a decision early on to spend one-third of his income on personal needs, one-third caring for others, and one-third on books.[4] His bedroom became so crowded with books that there was hardly room for him to sleep. He literally had to step over piles of books to get out the door!

The time he invested reading the Bible and great Christian authors soon had a considerable effect on his experience in several key areas, including baptism.

From his daily immersion in the Bible, he came to believe by March 1921 that baptism by sprinkling (which he had undergone as a boy in the Methodist church) was not scriptural. He studied the passages that dealt with baptism and concluded two things that were revolutionary for China in his day: First, he reasoned that baptism was for believers who understood what it meant to commit their lives to the lordship of Christ. The baptismal certificate he'd received as a child from the bishop was meaningless to him now that he'd been truly converted. He also recognized that the Bible portrays baptism as an experience of complete immersion; mere sprinkling does not convey the powerful New Testament image of coming up out of the pagan world system into newness of life.

God's timing is always perfect. Just as Watchman settled this crucial matter in his own mind, his mother approached him two days before Easter and characteristically blurted out, "I have given this much thought, my son. The next time you go to White Teeth Rock, I will accompany you. For there I must be baptized!"

With eyes wide, Watchman replied, "My dear mother! I have made the same decision myself. We will be baptized together!"

They left that same day for Miss Barber's mission; and early in the morning on Easter Sunday, March 28, 1921, Watchman and his mother were baptized by immersion in the golden waters of the Min River. "Please remember," he would later teach regarding baptism, "you are not the only one who is in the water. As you step down into the water, a whole world goes down with you. When you come up, you come up in Christ. For you, the world is submerged, put to death in the death of Christ and never to be revived. It is by baptism that you declare this, 'Lord, I leave my world behind. Your cross separates me from it forever!' "[5]

Soon after his immersion, Watchman returned to Foochow to talk with the pastor of his church. When the young idealist realized how different their views were concerning the importance of studying Scripture, Watchman resolved, "From that point on, I began to have doubts regarding the truths of the church in which he taught. I also realized that I must put man's authority aside, and I determined that from then on I would carefully study the Bible."[6]

This thorough study of God's Word led Watchman to two other eventful decisions. The first had to do with taking communion, the second with leaving his denomination. Throughout 1921, he dug steadily into the Scriptures to learn about these two areas. He discovered that believers should *often* come together to break bread in remembrance of Christ. But his denomination took Holy Communion only four times a year. Watchman faced the same question that Martin Luther and the other reformers asked four centuries earlier: *Should I obey the clear teaching of Scripture or submit to the authority of the church's tradition?*

In a sense, Watchman Nee's entire life was caught up in the Reformation-come-late to China. Like Luther, he looked around and saw a largely disinterested, carnal church moving away from orthodoxy, and he asked why it couldn't follow biblical guidelines. Had he spoken Latin, Watchman might have sounded the great Reformer's battle cry: "Sola Scriptura!"—the Bible only. As it was, he asked his close family friend, the Methodist bishop, about scriptural authority versus church authority.

"If the Bible says one thing and the church's tradition says another, which voice should I obey?" asked Watchman.

"Can you give me an example of this?" the bishop carefully replied.

"Well, let's consider Holy Communion. The Bible says in Acts 20:7 that the believers broke bread together on the first day of every week. And Acts 2 implies that communion was probably a daily experience. Why does our church make Holy Communion available only once every three months and allow only ordained clergy the privilege of serving it?"

"Well," came the cautious response, "because this has been our custom for many years."

"But where did the custom come from, sir? Is it scriptural?"

"Perhaps not, To-sheng. But the leaders of our church have gathered their wisdom and made these decisions."

"But sir, did they get their wisdom from God's Word?"

"Young man, your legalism could be your downfall. I fear what will happen to you if you pursue this course."

"With all respect, sir," said Watchman, "I fear what will happen to me if I do not obey the Scriptures."

Watchman began to go regularly to the private home of Leland Wang (Wilson's older brother and the future founder of the China Missionary Union) to remember the Lord together in Holy Communion along with Leland and his wife. "As long as I live," he wrote of that first meeting, "I will remember that experience. I was never so close to the heavens as on that night! All three of us could not help but weep! On that day we knew what it meant to worship and remember the Lord."[7]

Eventually, most of his friends and immediate family broke bread together every Lord's Day. Their hunger for all things scriptural grew daily, but perhaps not as quickly as the rumors of their "radical" behavior. Predictably, the news that the entire Nee family had been baptized by immersion and that many of them were meeting privately to take communion reached the ear of the district superintendent of the Methodist church. He came to visit the Nees and registered his concern about their actions.

Soon after he left, Watchman traveled to White Teeth Rock to ask Margaret Barber one question: "How do you feel about my name being in the Methodist church's book of life?"

Miss Barber answered with characteristic bluntness. "To-sheng, I am afraid that among the names in that book of life, many are dead and not a few are perishing." She thought for a moment and said, "If your name is recorded in the book of life in heaven, what good will an earthly book of life do you? And if your name is not recorded in the heavenly book of life, what will this earthly book of life profit you?"[8]

Watchman returned home and drafted a bold letter. Although his parents were concerned that the Western missionaries would be offended by it, they cosigned the letter that same afternoon. A few days later, the district superintendent read the following:

> *We have seen that sects are unscriptural and that denominationalism is sinful (see 1 Corinthians 1:10-13). Therefore, please remove our names from your book of life. We are doing this not because of any personal animosity, but simply because we wish to obey the Scriptures.*[9]

Four days after the letter was mailed, a steady stream of visitors began to appear at their doorstep: their pastor, bishop, superintendent, several missionaries, their school principal, and many others. Each brought the same message: "This step is too drastic for something as insignificant as mode of baptism. If you want to be immersed, we will make room for you."

The Nee's united response was straightforward and indicative of their new resolve to be biblical Christians.

"Baptism by immersion and leaving the denomination are not the point here. They are but two items among thousands that require our obedience. The real issue is whether or not we will obey the Scriptures."[10]

And so Watchman Nee left the church, but he was just beginning to understand what the real church was all about.

five

Nineteen-year-old Simon Meek could not remember a colder winter. It was almost impossible to keep warm on those dark days of 1922. Thirty miles from Foochow, on an extended visit to his relatives, Simon walked among the snow-topped coastal hills, embracing a tiny basket of dying charcoal embers to his chest. He needed some good news, and it came in the form of an urgent telegram from his best friend, Watchman Nee.

"Please return at once," it read. "God is doing a big work here, and we need you."[1]

By the time Simon arrived back, a great revival had begun in Foochow. When they weren't involved with schoolwork, large bands of young men, often sixty to eighty strong, organized and led by Watchman, set out on evangelistic missions. This nightly witnessing had a profound effect on their peers across the city; scores of male and female students were being wonderfully converted to Christ. Each of these, in turn, joined in the adventure, wearing their gospel shirts throughout the town, bearing the messages, "Believe in the Lord Jesus Christ" and "Jesus is coming."

The movement was energized by an evangelistic crusade led by a visiting preacher from Tientsin, Ruth Lee, a charismatic woman who would become an important influence on Watchman's life. Her powerful testimony and passionate speaking electrified her youthful audience.

Miss Lee told of the years she'd spent promoting atheism as the principal of a government school. In fact, her zeal for unbelief had been such that she searched out the Christian students, confiscated their Bibles, and publicly burned them. But without her knowledge, several of her students committed themselves to pray for her daily. Little by little, the prayers had their impact, and she came to Christ through the influence of her own students.

Miss Lee immediately resigned her civil post and started preaching. So many people were saved at her meetings that the decision was made to continue the gatherings even after she left for another city. Consequently, Watchman and a few of his more gifted friends found themselves preaching to larger crowds every evening. "For a year after my conversion," he said, "I had a lust to preach. It was impossible for me to stay silent. Preaching had become my very life."[2]

When the evening meetings in his hometown finally ran their course, Watchman and other believers often used weekends and holidays to travel to nearby villages and preach the gospel. Because these young evangelists were of the intellectual elite, almost everyone they met—from lowly coolies and soldiers to scholars and civic leaders—gave them respect and attention.

It became the custom of the traveling preachers to set up their operation in a borrowed church building, always dedicating one room for "prayer without ceasing." When the street evangelism and evening services began, each coworker took his turn in maintaining a twenty-four-hour prayer vigil.

Even during these early days, Watchman showed signs of what later would be the passion of his ministry: the work of discipling those who were being saved and the eventual planting of local churches. Many of his colleagues thought evangelism was the most important ministry they could do. "But God opened my eyes," he later testified, "to see that before long, He would raise up local churches in various parts of China. My vision was for the birth of local churches."[3]

About that time, Watchman made one of the most difficult decisions of his life. He had grown up in the same neighborhood as the Changs, a Christian family with several children. Charity Chang used to tag along after To-sheng everywhere he went. He had always viewed her as something of a friendly pest; but now in his early twenties, Watchman could hardly get her off his mind. Charity had blossomed into a beautiful young woman and an intellectual match for Watchman as well. Her faith was immature and her goals far from his own, yet Watchman would not give up his dream of marrying her. He had fallen deeply in love with Charity Chang.

Watchman tried everything he could think of to justify his love for her. He witnessed to her. He prayed for her. He labored to get her to commit her life to Christ. But Charity, unable to understand his spiritual passion, only laughed at his efforts. He was finding it almost impossible to preach, until one day he came across the verse "Whom have I in heaven but You? And there is none upon earth that I desire besides You" (Psalm 73:25).

I cannot preach this passage, he thought. He confessed that there was one person on earth who rivaled God for his love. "But I cannot give her up," he told the Lord. "I will make a deal with you, Father. Let me continue to love her and I will move far away from her. I will preach for You in the remote mountains of Tibet if necessary." For weeks, Watchman struggled through halfhearted sermons and avoided Psalm 73 with care.

Then one cold, February day, he could take it no longer. He returned to his room, opened his Bible, and cried out to God, "I will lay her aside! Never will she be mine!"[4] A supernatural peace flooded his spirit. That night, he wrote a song that Charity would not see for many years.

My precious Savior now I love
  Him only would I please.
For Him all gain a loss becomes
  And comfort holds no ease.

Thou art my comfort, gracious Lord
  I've none in heaven but Thee.
And who but Thee is there on earth
  With whom I love to be?

Though loneliness and trials come,
  My griefs I'd rise above.
This only would I ask Thee, Lord:
  Surround me with Thy love!

This heart-purifying experience happened about the same time Watchman decided that his senior year at Trinity College would be his final one of formal education. He and his friend, Faithful Luke, had been meeting three times a day with other students at Trinity for prayer, and they both believed that God was telling them the same thing. To the disappointment of most of their relatives and the school officials, these two bright, young men would not go on for further academic study and pursue lucrative careers as China's elite. Instead, they would take a vow of poverty and enter full-time Christian ministry.

It was prophesied of Jesus that He would be betrayed by His own friends (Zechariah 13:6).

Satan's most effective strategy has always been to attack us from within. Just as Watchman's ministry was gaining spiritual momentum, he was dealt a hard blow. Leland Wang and other close coworkers politely informed him that he was no longer welcome to worship with them. They also asked him not to attend the January holiday convention in Foochow that pulled together believers from all over the area, an event that Watchman had helped to organize.

The anti-Christian movement (an outgrowth of political China's hatred of all things "Western" after the Boxer Rebellion) was reaching a new peak to match the recent evangelistic activity—and much of the criticism was being focused on Watchman. "It is time for us to separate, To-sheng," said the Wangs. "It will be easier for us without you."

Watchman knew in his heart that the leaders (including many Western missionaries) were already being pressured by the government to compromise on several issues, and they knew Watchman would never do so. It was more expedient to move this "radical" preacher to the periphery of the movement. Even though he understood these motives, he was devastated by the betrayal of his friends.

Watchman moved from Foochow to Ma-hsien, a little fishing village not far from Miss Barber's mission, where Faithful Luke served the Lord. There he rented a small hut and threw himself into a deeper study of God's Word. He also laid out plans to publish a Christian magazine he called *Revival*. His hope was to write articles that would help new believers grow in the faith. But he was experiencing deep depression over the schism with his Foochow brothers and found it difficult to get started. Then Faithful Luke came to visit him from White Teeth Rock.

The two friends knew that Watchman was at an impasse and that no amount of human strategizing would bring a solution. So they did what had become natural for them after long months of practice. They prayed. By the shore of the Great China Sea, they agonized in prayer until they both felt they had a clear answer. They believed that God was saying to them, "Leave your problem with Me. You go and preach the Good News!"[5] Little did they know what God had in store for them just a few days later.

They received an urgent invitation from Faithful Luke's surrogate mother to come and preach in the pagan village where she worked as a midwife. The village of Mei-hwa was located on an island off the Chinese coast, and the two friends took five Christian brothers with them to saturate the area with the gospel. After a week of intense spiritual labor, there were no conversions. In fact, the townspeople ignored the energetic little band of believers and remained caught up in their own heathen celebrations.

Motivated by his frustration, Kuo-ching Lee, the youngest member of the band, shouted to a crowd of villagers, "What's wrong with you? Why don't you believe?"

"Oh, we do believe," said a spokesman. "We

believe in our great king, the god Ta-Wang. He never fails us."

When Kuo-ching asked what this meant, he was told that for the last 286 years, Ta-Wang had made the sun shine brightly for the people on his own festival day—which happened to be only two days away. Immediately, the good-intentioned young Christian saw his opportunity. He hastily announced, "Then I promise you, our God, who is the true God, will make it rain on the eleventh."

The crowd accepted his challenge quickly. "Say no more," they replied. "If there is rain on the eleventh, then your Jesus is indeed God. We will be ready to hear Him."

Watchman, who had been preaching in another locale when the bargain was struck, was dismayed when informed of its terms. Tempted to rebuke Kuo-ching for his rashness, he instead went to his knees for God's counsel.

"Father, have we gone too far?" he asked. "Should we leave this village now before Your name is maligned? Should we turn these people over to themselves?"

Where is the God of Elijah? came the response to his heartfelt prayer, reminding Watchman that the prophet had prayed down rain after three years of drought. The next day, during a time of prayer, the same question came back to confront his spirit. *Where is the God of Elijah?* Watchman was convinced that the Lord was promising the impossible: rain on a day that had not seen a drop of it in almost three centuries. In fact, he was so certain that he took Kuo-ching's challenge back to the streets, broadcasting it to all within the sound of his voice. The villagers were primed for a showdown between gods the following day.

The sun rising in a cloudless sky woke Watchman from a heavy sleep on the morning of January 11. He shielded his eyes from its bright rays and peered out the window. Unbelieving villagers scurried about their daily routines, busily preparing themselves for the day's pagan festivities.

"Lord," he prayed, "this doesn't look like the rain that You—" only to have his prayer cut short by a clear message that sounded in his mind: *Where is the God of Elijah?*

He dressed and joined his six companions at the breakfast table. There was apprehension on their faces when Watchman bowed to lead them in grace for the meal. "Father," he said, "please accept our prayer as a gentle reminder that You promised to answer the challenge of the demon-god today. Even though not a cloud appears in the sky, we trust in Your promise." Before he could say "Amen," the seven friends heard a few drops striking the tiles of their roof.

At the first sign of rain, several of the village children began to sing, "There is God; there is no Ta-Wang! There is God; there is no Ta-Wang!" But the older pagans were persistent. They hurried to their shrine and hoisted the heavy idol of their god onto a platform and carried him into the slippery street. As they loudly implored him to stop the rain and defeat this Jesus, the skies opened to a torrential downpour.

The scene outside Watchman's door was both exhilarating and comical. Where was the God of Elijah? He was unleashing a storm that morning the likes of which the people of Mei-hwa had never seen. The water had already reached the porch level of many houses and ran in deepening rivulets through the town. Watchman had a hard time not laughing when he saw how the bearers of the idol struggled to maintain their balance.

Where was the god Ta-Wang? He teetered on top of the platform, deaf to the cries of his worshippers. Just then, the bearers' legs were swept from beneath them, and the idol came crashing down to the pavement, breaking its head and left arm. The townspeople would have heard the cheers of Watchman's six coworkers if the roar of the storm hadn't been so loud.

The damaged statue was rushed into a home, where a pagan priest prayed over it for some time. When the storm finally abated, he emerged into the street proclaiming, "Today was the wrong day. The festival is to be held on the fourteenth at six in the evening."

Watchman knew that God heard the challenge, and he prayed confidently, "Lord, give us good weather until that hour. We have much to do." And for the next three and one-half days, the friends evangelized boldly under the clearest of skies. More than thirty villagers who had lived in darkness were publicly converted to Christ in beautiful weather right up to six o'clock on the evening of the fourteenth. At exactly the appointed hour, a mammoth storm that rivaled the first broke on the village. The resulting floods ended Ta-Wang's hold on the people for good.

The next day, Watchman returned to the mainland, strengthened in his faith by the lesson in God's power, which would serve him at the time of his arrest and imprisonment years later: No matter how hard the trial—even if your closest friends betray you—God is there and His work must go on.

six

"To-sheng," said Margaret Barber during one of Watchman's visits to the mission, "a small leaf on a tree can block out the full moon from one's sight."

"But, Miss Barber," he replied, "what are these leaves that I might remove them and stand fully in the light?"

"My young friend," she said, "if I prune your tree for you, you have learned nothing. You must face the truth within yourself."

He returned to his spartan existence in the small hut in Ma-hsien and spent long hours gazing at the Min River and reflecting on his life. His honest self-analysis eventually led him to realize two barriers that were keeping him from walking in full obedience, two small leaves that were blocking his view of God's perfect plan. The first problem area was his doubt regarding the faith.

After his graduation from Trinity College, Watchman left behind formal education and became a self-taught man in theology and the Scriptures. He read voraciously; but no matter how much he studied, he couldn't eliminate one fear that had pursued him for years: that a learned atheist or brilliant Bible critic could convince him that God's Word was unreliable. He was fearful that his resulting doubts would force him to turn away from the faith. Two incidents occurred that finally put his fear to rest.

The first was a story related to him by a simple tailor named Chen, who lived in Watchman's province. The only part of the Bible that Mr. Chen possessed was a single page he'd found, containing the last twelve verses of the Gospel of Mark. With no way of knowing that the most trustworthy early manuscripts didn't include these verses, thus making them unreliable to modern scholars, the little tailor treasured every word and came to know Christ Jesus personally through them. In fact, he decided after much prayer to test verse eighteen out in his own village. Even though he instinctively knew that God's gift of salvation in Christ was far more important than the sign gift of healing, he began a door-to-door campaign to prove the truth of verse eighteen. God honored his simple faith; and after the miraculous healing of one of his neighbors, he quietly returned to his shop to carry on with his tailoring and daily witnessing to his customers.

Watchman was deeply moved by this story and, after reflecting upon it, gave the same confident response whenever attacked by liberal scholars and critics of the faith: "Yes," he would calmly reply, "there is a great deal of reason in what you say—but I know my God. That is enough."[1]

Another incident not only cured him of any lingering doubts about the Christian faith, but led him to confront the second problem area that had kept him from walking in complete obedience. In a nearby village he met a recently converted farmer who faced a moral dilemma. His tiny rice field lay just above the hillside irrigation stream, and he worked hard to hand-pump the precious water up to his retaining tank. Time and again, his devious neighbor on the farm beneath him would sneak up the hill and tap into his water supply to irrigate his own two fields below.

Frustrated and angry, the Christian farmer went to his new church friends for advice. "Love your enemies and pray for those who persecute you," they quoted the Lord to him. After they prayed together, he knew what he had to do. "I must go the second mile," he said, and he returned to his farm for a labor of love. Early in the morning, he set up his machinery and pumped down enough water to take care of both fields belonging to his neighbor. Then in the afternoon, he pumped a supply for his own field.

Expecting revenge rather than love, his neighbor was deeply shaken. He walked up the hill to ask the Christian farmer why he had done such a gracious thing. After several such meetings, there were *two* Christian farmers living on that hillside.

The more Watchman observed God's Spirit working in the lives of those who met Christ through his evangelistic efforts, the less he doubted his faith. He knew he must now deal with the second barrier that was keeping him from being "filled to the measure of all the fullness of God": his connection to the Westernized (and often lifeless) form of quasi belief that passed for Christianity in his country.

All over China, the state of the institutional church had lapsed into lukewarm religious secularism. Denominational jealousies and prideful, compromised ecclesiastics had practically paralyzed the movement of the Spirit among the church system established by Western missionaries. As a result, the anti-Western, anti-Christian, nationalist sentiment was finding an attentive audience among many Chinese.

The corruption of the church was obvious, and yet Watchman saw large numbers of youth who were hungry for spiritual food—even though they were disillusioned with China's present form of Christianity. He became convinced that the answer could be found in a return to the pattern of God's truth found in the New Testament. He made a decision: Instead of capitalizing on the nationalist and antimissionary fervor of the day, he would maintain his Western contacts and devote his life to improving the spiritual quality of the Chinese Christian's life. "In God's work," Watchman said, "everything depends upon the kind of worker sent out and the kind of convert produced."[2]

His keen mind and passion for holiness made Watchman one of the few Christian intellectuals in China to see clearly the real problem of the church in his homeland: The faith of the believers was too shallow; they had no roots in the knowledge of God's Word. "My people are being destroyed for their lack of knowledge," cries the Lord (Hosea 4:6).

Watchman knew that somehow he had to make his countrymen aware that Christianity was more than the initial forgiveness of sins or the mere assurance of salvation. Immature believers needed to learn to overcome sin daily as a diligent "people of the Book." Jesus must be more than the One who gets us to heaven; He must be our very life on earth.

But how would he communicate this concept to his people? He was too busy preaching in the villages to do any serious writing. There was simply no time to put his thoughts into book form. "Besides," he thought, "I'm too young for such a project, and I have my whole life ahead of me." God was about to change his mind.

Watchman developed a severe cough and began waking up at night either sweating profusely or chilled to the bone. A visit to Dr. Wong revealed the bad news: tuberculosis. In fact, Watchman overheard the good doctor informing his nurse in an inner office: "Poor fellow! Do you remember the last case like his? He was dead in six months."[3]

At first, Watchman was gripped again by severe

depression. "Lord, how can this be happening?" he asked. "I have so many things to do for You. How can the end come when I've only just begun?"

After another battery of X rays had been taken, the doctor said, "You must not come to me anymore. I would only be stealing your money. There is no hope for you." Strangely enough, this news settled his spirit and galvanized him into action. Watchman reasoned, "If I am to die soon, Lord, let it be while I am writing down all the wonderful things the Holy Spirit has taught me from Your Word." Thus began his struggle to write *The Spiritual Man,* the magnum opus of his young life.

Eventually, his beloved friend, Faithful Luke, helped to move Watchman to Margaret Barber's care at White Teeth Rock. It was there that the high fever that often accompanies advanced tuberculosis seized him. He continued to push himself to write, often passing out over his notes, sometimes losing several days, of which he had no memory.

Once, he was bedridden, unconscious, for such a long period that word passed from his friends to churches throughout the province that he had died. He woke from that bout only to see the concerned face of Miss Barber looking down at him. Her brow still furrowed, she said with a gentle smile, "My dear To-sheng, Christ is the victor." When he was conscious, he could hear her quoting the Scriptures to him.

"When you have suffered in the body, you are done

with sin," she quoted Paul. "To-sheng, can you hear me?" she would ask. "His strength is made perfect in weakness. He is strengthening you on the inside."

"What you are experiencing is nothing new," she would whisper. "You are simply 'carrying about in your body the death of the Lord Jesus Christ.' Do not give up, my young friend. Christ is the victor."

The raging fever returned, but he refused to give in. Though his skin was hot to the touch, his spirit was hotter. Asking for more ink and paper, he wrote with abandon. One veteran nurse, who was visiting Miss Barber and did what she could for Watchman, burst into tears every time she entered the room and saw his pitiful condition. She confided in her friends, "I have seen many patients, but never one as sick as he is. I'm afraid he can live only three or four more days."[4]

When his colleagues tried to convince him that he would surely die at this pace, he shut himself up in his room and wrote with even more resolve. The disease got so bad that he could no longer breathe without pain while lying down. So he propped himself up in a high-backed chair, pressed his chest against the desk, and wrote on. He later testified, "Satan would come to me in that room and say, 'Since you will soon be dying, why not die in comfort rather than in pain?' I shouted back at him, 'The Lord wants me just like this; now get out of here!' "[5]

After four months of daily battling, all four volumes of *The Spiritual Man* lay in stacks on the table by his desk. Watchman prayed weakly, "Now let your servant depart in peace."

He was in the throes of death, and he knew it. So did his friend, Ruth Lee, who was visiting the mission. She gathered several believers from around the compound and led them in a three-day period of fasting and praying for Watchman. At the end of this time, as he lay on his bed laboring for breath, Watchman said that three verses clearly came to his mind: "By faith you stand" (2 Corinthians 1:24); "We walk by faith" (2 Corinthians 5:7); and "All things are possible to him who believes" (Mark 9:23). From that very moment, he believed that God had healed him. Meanwhile, the believers remained in prayer in a room below.

The testing of the truth of those verses came without delay. "By faith you stand," God's Word said to him. He slowly rose from his deathbed and dressed himself in clothing he'd not worn for a hundred and seventy-six days. Doing more wobbling than standing and drenched in sweat, Watchman remembered the words "Walk by faith." He took two steps and started to faint.

"Where do You want me to go?" he asked the Lord. The answer came: "Go downstairs to Sister Lee's room." With difficulty he crossed the room and opened the door to the stairwell. It was dangerously steep and looked impossible for him to negotiate. "All things are possible," whispered the Holy Spirit, and he began the descent. With each step he cried out, "Walk by faith; walk by faith!" With the twenty-fifth and final step, he realized total healing!

With tears in his eyes, Watchman walked briskly to Ruth Lee's room. When they opened the door to his knock, Miss Lee and his friends were speechless. For the better part of an hour, they all sat there quietly and smiled at him, unable to verbalize their joy. Finally, Watchman spoke and related the whole story of his healing. A time of sweet celebration and praise followed.

A few days later, at a Sunday morning worship service, Watchman Nee stood up and walked about for three hours, preaching God's Word with great power.

seven

By May 1928, with his health better than it had been in years, Watchman decided to move the base of his ministry to Shanghai. He had two good reasons. First, his coworker, Ruth Lee, lived there. She was not only a wonderful evangelist but an accomplished writer. Ten years his senior, Ruth offered to help him prepare his book for publication and advise him in launching his new magazine, *The Christian*.

The second reason was the city of Shanghai itself. Chinese believers often said of this wicked financial capital that "if God spared Shanghai, He owed an apology to Sodom and Gomorrah."[1] Watchman saw the potential for the gospel to make inroads quickly in this cesspool of sin. After all, had not the Lord Jesus more success among the notorious sinners of His day than among the respectable citizens?

Soon after he moved his headquarters to Shanghai, Watchman had another spiritual breakthrough that would affect all of his future speaking and writing. While making a few cosmetic changes on *The Spiritual Man*, he was struck by the pristine power of a passage in Romans that he had only thought he understood before. He recounted this powerful experience later in a book called *The Normal Christian Life:*

"For years after my conversion I had been taught that the way of deliverance was to reckon myself dead to sin and alive to God (Romans 6:11). I 'reckoned' from 1920 to 1927, and the more I did so, the more alive to sin I clearly was. I simply could not believe myself dead to sin. The problem was that no one had pointed out to me that knowing (verse 6) must precede reckoning (verse 11). For months I was troubled and prayed earnestly, reading the Scriptures and seeking light. I said to the Lord, 'If I cannot understand this—which is so fundamental—I will not preach anymore.'

"I remember one morning—how can I ever forget it!—I was sitting upstairs reading Romans and I came to the words: 'Knowing this, that our old man was crucified with Him, that the body of sin might be done away, that so we should no longer be in bondage to sin.' *Knowing* this! How could I know it? I prayed, 'Lord, open my eyes!' and then, in a flash, I saw.

"I had earlier been reading 1 Corinthians 1:30:

'You are in Christ Jesus.' I looked at it again. I thought, *the fact that I am in Christ Jesus is God's doing!* It was amazing! If Christ died, and that is a certain fact, and if God put me into Him, then I must have died, too. All at once I saw my oneness with Christ: that I was in Him, and that when He died I died. My death to sin was a matter of the past and not of the future.

"I jumped from my chair and ran downstairs to the young man working in the kitchen. 'Brother,' I said, seizing him by the hands, 'do you know that I have died?' I must admit he looked puzzled. 'What do you mean?' he exclaimed; so I went on: 'Do you not know that Christ has died? Do you not know that I died with Him? Do you not know that my death is no less truly a fact than His?'

"Oh, it was so real to me! I felt like shouting my discovery through the streets of Shanghai. From that day to this I have never for one moment doubted the finality of that word: 'I have been crucified with Christ; it is no longer I who live, but Christ who lives in me.' "[2]

This remarkable revelation proved to be a milestone in his life. From this moment on, it became almost impossible to offend him. Why should he retaliate when criticized? He had already died to self-promotion. He made the decision never to defend himself and never to argue when personally rebuked.

As usual, the test came quickly. One day, a younger

coworker confronted him in the presence of several believers. A friend of Watchman's observed the ugly scene and later told the story:

> *The man pointed his finger and pounded*
> *his fist, rebuking Watchman for almost four*
> *hours. But he sat calmly in his chair, without*
> *changing expression. At times, he would even*
> *nod his head in agreement. As unfair as the*
> *accuser was, I knew that Watchman was sub-*
> *mitting himself to this circumstance God had*
> *allowed.[3]*

Little by little, he was becoming a person of the cross. With a new sense of peace, he learned to accept every problem that came his way as another opportunity to grow spiritually. About this time he wrote the following poem:

> *Not by gain our life is measured,*
> *   But by what we've lost it's scored;*
> *It's not how much wine is drunken,*
> *   But how much has been outpoured.*
> *He who treats himself severely*
> *   Is the best for God to gain;*
> *He who hurts himself most dearly*
> *   Most can comfort those in pain.*

Watchman was finally realizing what Margaret Barber had been trying to teach him for years: that the only place where a believer grows is in the valley of the shadow of death. To that end, the Lord had another valley for Miss Barber's most extraordinary pupil to cross.

He was visiting his beloved mentor for a few days when the fever that had plagued him a few years earlier returned with a vengeance. He had exhausted himself by preaching at every opportunity, and with the return of winter came a violent cough and something worse, although he was not yet aware. Watchman had contracted a heart disease, angina pectoris, a malady that would stalk him for the rest of his life.

In severe pain and suffering again from cold sweats, he left White Teeth Rock and journeyed home to Foochow to seek the solace of his family. When Peace Nee saw him, she feared that he would not live long. She put him to bed immediately, but early the next morning he rose and left the house. Few of the townspeople even recognized him as he shuffled through the streets with the help of a walking stick. His hair disheveled, his eyes underlined by dark circles, and his face gaunt with a ghostly pallor, Watchman hardly resembled the virile young man with the bright future who had graduated from Trinity College not long before.

He had not gone far when he crossed the path of one of his favorite professors from Trinity. The teacher almost walked past him, then stopped and stared impolitely for a moment. Catching himself, the older man gathered himself and asked, "Young

Mr. Nee, would you care to join me in the shop across the bridge for some tea?" Tempted to decline self-consciously, Watchman accepted the invitation and soon found himself sitting in silence across the table from his old law professor.

While the teacher continued to take a visual inventory, obviously finding it difficult to express his concern, Watchman felt Satan sniping at him from the shadows of the tea shop.

"You had a bright future," the enemy seemed to whisper in his ear. "Full of possibilities, and you gave it up to serve God. That was splendid. But then you had a promising ministry in which, with your gifts, you were assured of success, and that, too, you threw away. For what?"

Watchman squirmed in his chair, not taking his eyes off the professor, and the voice in his head continued. "You gave up so much; what have you gained? A Christian should look happy, satisfied, and assured. Take a look at yourself; you are none of these!"

The man across the table took one more up-and-down survey of Watchman's pathetic frame and said, "What is this? We thought so much of you at Trinity and had hopes that you would achieve something great. Do you mean to say that you are truly like this?"

For a moment, Watchman wilted even further under the man's piercing stare. Tears came to his eyes as he realized that humanly speaking, his professor was right. He was a sorry figure who inspired more pity than praise. With his health broken again and the future looking bleak, he surrendered to the oncoming tears. Embarrassed for his student, the Trinity don rose without looking at Watchman and excused himself with, "I will leave you alone."

"Alone," he thought, watching the man leave. The debilitating self-pity within him began to turn to spiritual steel. "I am *not* alone," he said out loud. "Greater is He that is in me than he that is in the world. If God is for me, who then can be against me?" A passage from 1 Peter rushed back to him: "If you are insulted because of the name of Christ, you are blessed, for the Spirit of glory and of God rests on you. If you suffer as a Christian, do not be ashamed, but praise God that you bear that name" (1 Peter 4:14,16).

Watchman got up to walk home. He still needed the cane, but the shuffle was less pronounced. "I will not despair," he said to the Lord, turning onto the street that led to his parents' house. "For the Spirit of God and of glory rests on me. My professor thinks that I am wasting my life, but even if I die today, my life would only have begun. Lord, I praise you that I have chosen the best way."[4]

His mother convinced him to seek the counsel of doctors. Their unanimous prescription was a forced rest in the healthier climate of Kuling Mountain. After a six hundred mile boat trip up the Yangtze River, Watchman found himself at the base of Kuling, observing the steep hill stairway that ascended thirty-five hundred feet up the mountain to his summer residence. "When I can descend that stairway on my own, I will be ready to leave this place," he vowed silently. A sedan chair carried his spent body to a tiny house, where he would sleep for days at a time.

As he gradually recuperated, he took short walks to scenic overlooks that showed off the verdant Yangtze Valley. On one of these occasions, he was arguing again with God about the state of his health. Becoming more obsessed daily with his physical condition, he exclaimed, "Lord, you simply must restore me to full health. There is so much work to be done!"

The answer came quickly to his spirit: "This is my affair," said the Lord. "You trust Me and drop it!" But day after day he ambled across mountain paths arguing with God. "Father, how much longer must I wait? So few have heard about You, and those few must be discipled. When will I be well?" That same inner voice spoke to him once more: "You must trust Me, my son. You must let the matter go and trust Me."

This time, Watchman was immediately repentant. He found a hefty stick by the path and, kneeling down, drove it as deeply into the ground as he could. "Lord, I do trust you!" he cried out. "I have dropped the matter of my healing here!" But no sooner had he risen to return to his cottage than a wave of anxiety and nausea swept over him. That old cloud of despair began to descend upon his spirit, and he instinctively started in to argue with God once more.

Before he fell into the trap, however, he caught

himself. *What am I doing?* he thought. *It's the enemy again.* Angry with his own dullness, Watchman turned back to the spot where he had impaled the stake, and, dramatically pointing to it, he announced for Satan and the world to hear, "Lord, I dropped the matter of my healing here. I refuse to take it up again!"[5] As far as the records show, he never did.

In fact, when he forgot about his predicament, two wonderful things happened. His health improved and he had the mental energy to rethink his growing faith. He realized that God was simply giving him the opportunity to become more of a person of the Cross. "When I first came to the Lord," he wrote later, "I had my own conception of what a Christian was. I thought a true Christian should smile from morning to night. If at any time he shed a tear, he had ceased to be victorious. I thought, too, that a Christian must be unfailingly courageous. If under any circumstances he showed the slightest sign of fear, he had fallen short of my standard. But when I read Paul's autobiographical letter, 2 Corinthians, I saw that he was 'sorrowful,' often 'perplexed,' shedding 'many tears,' and even in 'despair of life itself.' I discovered that Paul was a man, and the very sort of man that I knew."

Out of this experience, 2 Corinthians 4:7 became a theme passage for Watchman's life: "We have this treasure in earthen vessels, to show that the transcendent power belongs to God and not to us." Another piece had been added to his spiritual backbone, and his resolve never to be surprised by any circumstance that God allowed to come his way was stronger than ever. As usual, the Lord's timing for such a lesson was perfect. No sooner was he strong enough to descend the mountain steps than he received the news that his beloved mentor, Margaret Barber, had died.

She died at the age of sixty-four in relative obscurity at White Teeth Rock. Few outside the mission compound had ever seen her. But the students that she mentored, Faithful Luke, Simon Meek, Leland Wang, Watchman Nee, and others, changed the face of Christianity in the most populated country in the world. Watchman wrote of her, "She was one who was very deep in the Lord, and in my opinion, the kind of fellowship she had with the Lord and the kind of faithfulness she expressed to the Lord are rarely found on this earth."[6]

At the time of her death, Miss Barber had only two possessions: her character and her Bible. She took the one to heaven with her and left the other to Watchman. When he opened the well-worn book, he found a handwritten prayer that summed up her remarkable relationship to the Lord: "O God, grant me a complete and unrestrained revelation of my own self."

Margaret Barber was both the most honest and humble person he had ever known. She taught him better than anyone else how to pay more attention to the quality of his inner life than the visible success of his outward ministry; that "to be" was more important than "to do." Because of her steady influence, honesty and humility would also characterize Watchman for the rest of his life.

eight

As the crowd gathered for Sunday morning worship at the Hardoon Road church in Shanghai, Watchman observed the congregation from his wooden seat at the side of the platform. As usual, he had prepared his message with extraordinary care for the specific needs of his listeners. Lately he was aware of how hard they were working at living the impossible Christian lifestyle only to find themselves fighting spiritual dryness and discouragement.

He stood and walked to the corner of the lectern, leaning on it casually, looking from face to face among the crowd. He began his sermon.

"I will tell you a parable about a centipede I knew once," he announced brightly. His audience was already attentive. "One day, as the centipede was about to go for a walk, it examined its legs to consider which one should move first. Should the left leg move first or the right one? How about the eighth leg or the tenth? The centipede was a victim of self-paralysis, stuck there trying to decide which leg to move. The problem of the mind became a problem of the practice."

As was his custom, Watchman paused and waited for the half-finished parable's truth to sink in. "But if you don't know which leg to move first, how can you ever begin a journey?" asked Wu-chen Chang, three rows back on the right side.

"By giving no consideration to the problem in the first place," answered Watchman, seeing his opportunity to teach a great truth. "We all work too hard at being religious. God is much easier to live with than we are with ourselves. As Paul said to his friends in Ephesus, simply 'walk in His love.' "

"But what happened to the centipede?" came a question from his left. Watchman turned to engage the open expression of an eight-year-old girl named Mary Yu. Her winsome smile warmed his heart as he replied.

"Eventually, the sun came up," he said, his eyes shining with enthusiasm. "Without thinking, our little centipede ran out to see the sunrise without considering which leg to move first. It forgot about how to walk and simply walked. When the problem of the mind was gone, the problem of the practice also disappeared." Watchman stepped down from the platform and walked among his congregation, warming to the task.

"The truth is that the more you try to deal with inner dryness, depression, and flatness, the more you cannot overcome them. These things become an issue because we make them an issue. If you forget about them and let them go, they will disappear."

"But doesn't this 'forgetting business' contradict what you've taught us before?" asked John Chang, his coworker and friend sitting in the front row. "Haven't you instructed us many times to fight against the devil?"

"No, my dear friend," said Watchman gently. "Resisting the devil is far different from trying to fight him on your own. You will lose that battle every time. The enemy can only be overcome by the blood of the Lamb (Revelation 12:10). You resist him by hiding in Christ. Besides, resisting the devil is not the same thing as spiritual dryness. You conquer discouragement and the tyranny of impossible religious expectations by forgetting about them. True faith is not about you trying; it's about you *dying*. We all must learn to walk in His love."

As always, the crowd was caught up in this dialogue sermon between the shepherd and his flock. "Pastor," John Chang said, "we know that your words are true. But how can we learn to walk in His love?"

"Beloved," Watchman answered, measuring the room, "before my conversion, I devoted my life to accumulating material things: clothing, high marks in school, money, and so forth. And for years after I was saved, I was still in the habit of accumulating things—even though they were now spiritual things: godliness, high morals, wisdom, and patience. But I was still groping in a kind of darkness, seeking to amass as personal possessions the virtues I felt should make up the Christian life—and getting nowhere in the effort."[1]

Many of his listeners nodded their heads in understanding. They were weary of trying to be good. He ended his message with an impassioned plea: "Don't you see, my friends? I'd been accumulating spiritual things and was no better for it. Stay away from that dead-end road. It will paralyze you like the centipede. Then, one day I was reading Philippians 1:19-21." It was not unusual for him to quote from memory entire passages for them. He did so now:

> I know that through your prayers and the
> help given by the Spirit of Jesus Christ, what
> has happened to me will turn out for my
> deliverance. I eagerly expect and hope that I
> will in no way be ashamed, but will have
> sufficient courage so that now as always
> Christ will be exalted in my body, whether
> by life or by death. For to me, to live is
> Christ and to die is gain.

" 'For to me, to live is Christ.' " he repeated. "You see it now, don't you? We labor all our lives to be Christ-like, only to find that such a goal was impossible from our first effort. While we struggle to be more Christ-like and grow more discouraged daily when it doesn't happen, He simply wants to live out His life within us. For to me, to live is Christ. It is Christ Himself living through us; speaking, witnessing, fathering, befriending, writing and singing through us!"

Many in the congregation could hardly breathe. They knew instinctively that what they were hearing was the key to Christian living. For several of them, this would begin to release them from the grind of working to earn God's favor and set them on the excellent path of learning to live in His grace.

"O the emptiness of things!" Watchman cried. "When they are not an expression of His life within us, they are dead. I don't want to be more like Jesus; I want Jesus to be Himself living within me. Once I saw this truth, it was the beginning of a new life for me. From here on, your daily life can be summed up in one phrase, 'Walk in His love.' "

The sermon completed, the congregation sat in silence, contemplating the wisdom they had heard. A few rose discreetly and slipped to the back of the hall, but most sat bowed and gave the Holy Spirit time to engrave the lesson on their hearts.

So ended another midsummer worship service in the little church on Hardoon Road. It seemed hard to believe that just six months earlier this marvelous fellowship had not even existed.

Watchman had been regularly attending a Bible study in the home of a new friend, Miss Peace Wang, a graduate of Nanking Girls' Seminary and a colleague of Ruth Lee's. Years earlier, as a militant atheist, Ruth Lee had done everything possible to destroy Peace's immature faith. But both young women made radical commitments to the Lordship of Christ and became highly effective itinerant evangelists. It was not unusual for them to speak to crowds numbering more than a few thousand and to see several hundred pray for salvation.

Still, something was missing from their ministries when Ruth invited her friend to move her base of operations to Shanghai. Ruth already had coaxed Watchman into relocating there so that she could help him to publish his magazine, *The Christian,* which was growing daily in readership. When Peace Wang met Watchman Nee, she found the something that was missing.

"We must do more than evangelism," Watchman passionately stated, as the Bible study group assembled in Peace Nee's home late in the winter. "Our Lord poured His life into the twelve disciples for three and one-half years before He told them to go into all the world. We are winning people to Christ without pouring our lives into them."

"But, Brother Nee," said Peace Wang, "the Bible tells us to do the work of an evangelist."

"Yes, friend, but next to the Lord, the greatest evangelist of all said, 'We came to share with you

not only the gospel of God but our lives as well' "
(1 Thessalonians 2:8), he quoted the apostle Paul.
"The believers in China are shallow and rootless.
They are clouds without rain. After they come to
Christ, someone must help them to grow deeper."

With this resolve, what became perhaps the finest
church movement in China's brief Christian history
had its humble beginning. Watchman, Ruth, Peace
and John Wang dedicated themselves to a broader
definition of evangelism than their predecessors.
They were convinced that if they followed the prim-
itive, New Testament pattern of evangelism, a strong
local church whose members were being discipled
daily would be the result.

The church in Shanghai began to grow by word
of mouth. It had an irrepressible quality of life and
spirit, and soon people throughout the province were
talking about it. From the beginning, however,
Watchman had a fear of popularity. He dreaded the
"life out of focus" that seemed common among those
who were well received.

"My destiny is to be either raptured or martyred,"
he confided to his friends, adding, "I refuse to be
admired." And to that end, he worked hard to simplify
his life and ministry and to deflect any praise that
came his way.

His desire for unity among all Christians led him
to give the most general terms to every phase of his
work. He called the building for their worship services the assembly hall; he named his magazine *The*

Christian, spoke of the Christian life as "the way," and referred to Christians simply as "believers." He would never think of anyone as an Anglican, Methodist, or Baptist, for denominationalism was anathema to him. And yet, he made an innocent mistake that caused his work to be labeled with a name that has stuck even to this day.

Watchman was drawn to a Brethren hymnbook entitled *Hymns for the Little Flock.* He translated the songs for his congregation and inadvertently left the title on his new church hymnals. Missionary friends took to the name quickly and began to circulate it in their travels. Even though Watchman changed the title as soon as he heard that people were calling the Hardoon Street church, the "Little Flock," it was too late. As much as he detested labels, his ministry would forever be known as the Little Flock movement.

It wasn't long before influential Christian leaders in England picked up news about God's working among the Little Flock. In particular, Charles Barlow, a member of the elitist, ultraconservative "London Group" of Brethren heard about Watchman. He decided to pay him a call when he came to Shanghai on business in the winter of 1931. After a lively ten-day visit, Mr. Barlow wrote home to his Brethren friends about the believers in China.

"Watchman Nee is undoubtedly the outstanding man among them. He is far beyond all the rest. He is only twenty-eight but has a good education and is possessed of marked ability."[2]

The visitor was most impressed by Watchman's knowledge of the Bible and the way he communicated it to his congregation. He observed their attentiveness to the young pastor's words and his passion for feeding them straight from the Scriptures' depths. He was daily leading them into spiritual waters as yet uncharted by many of Barlow's acquaintances back in London.

In fact, it was about this time that Watchman's mother came to hear her son preach at a Bible conference in Shanghai. His own rigorous spiritual regimen that he had kept up for more than ten years (studying through the New Testament at least once a month and memorizing huge sections of the Old Testament, while often praying up to four hours a day) took her out of her depth during his first message. After a few days of listening to him, this godly woman, a fine student of Scripture herself, confessed, "What my son preached was too deep and I could not understand it; and I was too proud to ask questions; but beholding their life, I was bowed to the ground in respect."[3]

Charles Barlow was not too proud to ask. His enthusiasm about Watchman's ministry was boundless. "What is the goal of your work here?" he asked, including, "that I might inform my brethren in England."

"To supply spiritual milk to the young believers," responded Watchman, "and solid food to the older ones. We especially stress the salvation of the cross.

But we are even more concerned with the spiritual condition of the believers."

"Then you understand the dangers of spending most of your time trying to win the lost," said Barlow. "My friends will be encouraged by that—as well as by your care for rightly dividing the word of truth."

"We preach all of God's truth and not just a portion of it," said Watchman evenly. "As to the errors of modernism, we strive to warn God's children of its dangers."

Mr. Barlow smiled warmly, inspiring Watchman to continue. "You know that the Bible is our only standard. We are not afraid to preach the pure Word of the Bible, even if men oppose; but if it is not the Word of the Bible, we could never agree even if everyone approved."[4]

The visitor from London could not have been more glowing in the reports that he sent back home. The stories about this indigenous group of Chinese Christians sent a wave of spiritual electricity through the London Group of Brethren, so much so that by October 1932, a deputation team of English-speaking Brethren (representing Great Britain, Australia, and the United States) boarded a ship in England and sailed for China.

The stage was set for Watchman's understanding of global faith to be enlarged.

nine

The eight visitors arrived at Hardoon Road just as Watchman began his morning message. Brand-new chairs had been purchased for the occasion, and Charles Barlow silently led his delegation into the row reserved for them.

Watchman had already introduced his sermon topic, and most of the worshippers were busily turning Bible pages to find the text. As he watched the guests take their seats, he made a quick decision. Believing the homily he'd prepared for his flock to be too important to interrupt for the late-arriving team, he continued his message.

"In John 8:23, our beloved Lord said to His Jewish congregation, 'You are from beneath; I am from above; you are of this world; I am not of this world.' I wish us to note especially here the use of the words 'from' and 'of.' The Greek word in each case is *ek*, which means 'out of' and implies origin. *Ek tou kosmos* is the expression used: 'from,' or 'out of this world.' So the sense of the passage is: 'Your place of origin is beneath; my place of origin is above. Your place of origin is this world; my place of origin is not this world.' The question is not, Are you a good or bad person? but, What is your place of origin? We do not ask, Is this thing right? or, Is that thing wrong? but, Where did it originate? It is origin that determines everything. 'That which is born of the flesh is flesh; that which is born of the Spirit is spirit' " (John 3:6).

Barlow turned slightly toward Dr. Powell of California and whispered, "Can you believe this man's depth? And he's only warming up!" He leaned forward in his seat, his gaze following Watchman back and forth across the platform. "If nothing else good happens on this entire trip," he thought, "to hear this man preach has been worth our journey."

Watchman continued, "So when Jesus turns to His disciples, He can say, using the same Greek preposition, 'If you were of the world (*ek tou kosmos*), the world would love its own: but because you are not of the world, but I chose you out of the world, therefore the world hates you' (John 5:19). Here we have the same expression, 'not of the world,' but in addition we have another and more forceful expression, 'I chose you out of the world.' In this latter instance there is a double emphasis. As before there is an *ek,* 'out of,' but in addition to this, the verb 'to choose,' *eklego,* itself contains another *ek.* Jesus is saying that His disciples have been 'chosen out, out of the world.'

"There is this double *ek* in the life of every believer. Out of that vast organization called the *kosmos,* out of all the great mass of individuals belonging to it and involved in it, out, clean out of all of that, God has called us. And so comes the title 'church,' *ekklesia,* God's 'called-out ones.' If you are a called one, then you are a called-out one.

"As the people of God we have two titles: If we look back at our past history we are *ekklesia,* the church; but if we look to our present life in God we are the Body of Christ, the expression on earth of Him who is in heaven. From the standpoint of God's choice of us, we are out of the world; but from the standpoint of our new life, we are not of the world at all but from above. On the one hand, we are a chosen people, called and delivered out of the world system. On the other, we are a regenerate people, utterly unrelated to that system because by the Spirit we are born from above."

Watchman measured his audience and delivered the crux of the message: "As the people of God, heaven is not only our destiny but our origin."

Not wanting to take their eyes from the speaker, now and again one of the visitors glanced at his neighbor with a look that communicated his enthusiasm for the message. Watchman announced with joy, "This is an amazing thing, that in you and me there is an element that is essentially otherworldly. The life we have as God's gift came from heaven and never was in the world at all. It has no correspondence with the world but is in perfect correspondence with heaven; and though we must mingle with the world daily, it will never let us settle down and feel at home there.

"My beloved friends, have you, like Lot, pitched your tent toward Sodom? Have you so deeply buried your tent stakes that you will not be able to move out in the morning when our Lord returns? Do you feel too much at home in this world, a world that Jesus told us lies in the lap of the evil one? Listen to what God's Word tells us about our position to the world around us." In a forceful and rapid-fire delivery, Watchman quoted from memory the following verses:

> *"Love not the world or anything in the world. If anyone loves the world, the love of the Father is not in him. For everything in the world—the cravings of sinful man, the lust of his eyes and the boasting of what he has and does—comes not from the Father but from the world. The world and its desires pass away, but the man who does the will of God lives forever" (1 John 2:15-17).*
> *"Don't you know that friendship with the world is hatred toward God? Anyone who chooses to be a friend of the world*

becomes an enemy of God" (James 4:4).
"Greater is He that is in you than he
that is in the world" (1 John 4:4).
"Therefore come out from them and be sep-
arate,' says the Lord" (2 Corinthians 6:17).

"Do not be discouraged, dear ones; together we can learn how to stop living between two worlds. Let us not forget," said the pastor at Hardoon Road, "we serve the One who has 'overcome the world,' and so we can also be 'overcomers.' I want each of you to consider two things before we come together again: where your life intersects too closely with the world, and whether or not you are willing to come out from it. Now let's pray."

After his prayer, Watchman led the congregation in a song from the Little Flock hymnal and a number of the people dispersed. But most stayed behind to participate in a meal carried in for the guests.

At the table, many of the locals shared a good laugh at the expense of the delegation when they observed their remedial skill with chopsticks. Still, a bridge was being built between two very different cultures, and Watchman sensed the significance of the occasion. When they had finished the meal, he stood and spoke.

Our differences are obvious and many.
We rely on two sticks for eating; you are
lost without your knife and fork.

Good-natured laughter rippled through the audience.

You are white-skinned; we are more colorful.

Another laugh of equal magnitude ensued.

You are a short people; we are much taller.

At this, the crowd erupted with laughter, because the visitors towered over almost every one of their hosts except for Watchman, who was taller than each of the guests.

He paused for a moment and continued,

But one thing we have in common with you,

and his eyes became soft with humility.

We are sinners who need a Savior in Jesus Christ. Let us speak of our love for Him.

At this, several members of the flock along with the foreign delegation entered into a time of spontaneous testimony, relating what God's Son had done for them. The mutual joy they experienced in one another's confessions that day was tangible. Afterward, when all of his congregation had left for their homes, Watchman found himself surrounded by the deputation team, who began plying him with questions. W. J. House of Australia was the first to speak: "Pastor Nee, the message you gave us from God's Word was inspiring, but I couldn't help feeling that you were not done speaking when you brought it to a close. Am I right, or am I wrong?" he asked.

"You are right," responded Watchman, bringing a smile to the visitor's face, "and you are wrong." Mr. House looked confused. Amused at the visitor's perplexity, Watchman finished his thought.

"You were right because God's Word is never done speaking. In fact, it is following my friends into their homes even now and doing its work in their hearts and minds. But you were wrong when you sensed that my words were not completed. On the contrary, I probably said more than I should have."

Charles Barlow joined in. "But Pastor, you only told them to come out of the world. You did not tell them how to live in it."

"Dear Brother Barlow," Watchman replied, "before we put their boats in the water, I want them to spend a few days considering the water that is already in their boats."

"As usual, you are too deep for me," said Barlow, smiling.

"The water is deeper than both of us," said Watchman, returning the smile.

"We will not be able to hear your next sermon," Mr. Mayo of Great Britain interjected. "What will your topic be?"

"My topic is always the Lord Jesus, and He often surprises me. But my plans are to speak on 1 Corinthians 1:30, in which Brother Paul makes a striking twofold statement: that God Himself has placed us in Christ, and that Christ has been 'made unto us wisdom from God, righteousness and sanctification and redemption.'

"This word 'redemption' is the key one and has a great deal to do with the world. The Israelites, you will recall, were 'redeemed' out of Egypt, which is for us a figure of this world under satanic rule. 'I am Jehovah,' God said to Israel, 'and I will redeem you with a stretched out arm.' So God brought them out, setting a barrier of judgment between them and Pharaoh's pursuing host, so that Moses could sing of Israel as 'the people which Thou has redeemed.' "

"But what does this mean for us?" asked W. J. House.

"It means everything to us," rejoined Watchman. "If God has placed us *in Christ,* then because Christ is altogether out of the world, we too are altogether out of the world. He is now our sphere; and being in Him, we are by definition out of that other sphere." He paused momentarily, waiting to see understanding on their faces; then he quoted Colossians 1:13,14.

" '*The Father* delivered us out of the power of darkness, and translated us into the Kingdom of His dear Son; in whom we have our redemption.'

"Can you see why this is such good news?" he exclaimed joyfully. "If God has placed us in Christ and Christ is 'made unto us redemption'—then that means that *within us* God has set Christ Himself as the barrier to resist the world. We have all made our pathetic attempts to resist the world and failed miserably. The reason that we failed is that the effort was impossible from the beginning. But trying to be unworldly is not only impossible, it's unnecessary. Christ alone is our barrier to the world, and we need nothing more. And because of Christ, the world cannot reach me.

"This is exactly what all Christians must learn before the tyranny of unrealistic expectations discourages them. We do not need to try to resist or escape the system of things. If I look within myself for something with which to overcome the world, I instantly find everything within me crying out for that world; while if I struggle to detach myself from it, I simply become more and more involved.

"But let the day once come when I recognize that within me Christ is my redemption and that in Him I am altogether 'out.' That day will see the end of my struggling. I shall simply tell Him that I can do nothing at all about this 'world business,' but thank Him with all my heart that He is my Redeemer. And maybe by next week," he said, his eyes bright with hope, "my brothers and sisters will begin to live this truth."

"Pastor Nee," said Charles Barlow, "you simply must come to England to speak to the brethren there."

"Your intentions are kind," replied Watchman, "but what makes you think that they would receive me any better than our Lord Himself was received? Jesus said, 'All men will hate you because of me.' When the world meets in us a natural human honesty and decency, it appreciates this and is ready to pay us due respect. But as soon as it meets that in us which is not of ourselves, namely the person of Christ, its hostility is at once aroused.

"Show the world the fruits of Christianity, and it will applaud; show it Christianity and it will oppose it vigorously. For let the world evolve as it will, it can never produce one Christian. A so-called Christian civilization like yours," he said to Barlow, a man he had come to love, "gains the recognition and respect of the world. The world can tolerate that; it can even assimilate and utilize that. But Christian life—the life of Christ in the believer— that it hates; and wherever the world meets it, it will oppose it to the death."

"Then are you telling us that we should drop out of this world to live the life of an ascetic?" asked Barlow.

"No, my dear friend," said Watchman, without the slightest hint of condescension. "On the contrary again, Christians have a vital place in the world. Our blessed Savior said to His Father, 'I do not pray that You take them from the world, but that You keep them safe from the evil one.' That is the very problem with most of Christendom. Incurably religious people try to overcome the world by getting out of it. As Christians, that is not our attitude at all. Right here is the place where we are called to be overcomers. Created distinct from the world, we accept with joy the fact that God has placed us in it. The life of Christ within us is all the safeguard we need. For where there is true life, what fear is there of mixture with the world?"

Knowing something of his listeners' backgrounds, Watchman added, "I have no interest in Christian societies that build legalistic barriers around themselves to keep unstained from the world. Jesus Christ is our only effective barrier against the world. I have every interest in building His life into the believers He has placed in my charge."

As if he'd only half-heard Watchman's words, Charles Barlow pressed his earlier point. "You simply must come to England. You will be such a blessing to us."

"I will come," replied Watchman to the later astonishment of many of his colleagues. "But I will not be such a blessing."

At the age of thirty, for the first time in his life, Watchman Nee left his homeland. The English hospitality was so warm for the initial days of his visit there, that it seemed his earlier premonition in China had been wrong. The London Group of Brethren invited him to all of their gatherings and enjoyed introducing this "interesting young man from China" to their members. In retrospect, Watchman felt that he was mostly a novelty to them and not taken very seriously because of his youthful appearance.

After the novelty wore off, he found himself learning much by listening and observing. From the beginning he was impressed by the breadth of their knowledge on a variety of religious subjects. But Watchman was repeatedly disturbed by their spiritual arrogance when he heard revealing comments like, "Is there anything in the field of spiritual revelation that we Brethren do not have? To read what other Christians have written is a waste of time. What do any of them have that we have not got?"[1]

It was several days later at a Bible conference that his true feelings about the spiritual complacency of his hosts came to the surface. When given the rare opportunity to add his comments to a lengthy doctrinal discussion, Watchman rose to his full height and spoke with conviction.

"My dear brothers, your understanding of the truth is vast, but in my country it would avail you only this much," he said, lifting his right hand and snapping his fingers, "if when the need arose you could not cast out a demon." He later commented to Charles Barlow, "Your people have wonderful light, but oh so little faith."[2]

Of course, Watchman's candor offended many of the Brethren and a parting of the ways seemed inevitable. But for the time being, an open confrontation between his ministry in China and the London Group was put off. Watchman returned home maintaining an uneasy relationship with the Brethren movement.

ten

Watchman could not have returned to China at a more exciting time. It was the spring of 1934, and under Chiang Kai-shek's aggressive leadership, China was experiencing a brief but unparalleled boom in transportation. New road systems, railways, and even air travel were opening the country up, and Watchman's coworkers in Shanghai joined in his vision to saturate as many provinces as possible with the gospel message.

Even though Watchman's passion lay in the areas of teaching and discipleship, he sensed the spirit of the times and decided to take this opportunity to reach his homeland for Christ. Gathering the Shanghai believers together, he challenged them to evangelize their countrymen, even if it meant accepting job offers to other cities where they could make their new homes evangelistic centers.

"Because you are not witnessing," he told them, "many have not heard the gospel. They will be eternally separated from God. What a consequence of our apathy!" His voice raised in pitch and intensity.

"It is absolutely impossible for a person to have light and not to shine. As there is no tooth that does not chew, no fountain that does not flow, so there is no life that does not beget life. Whoever has no interest to help people repent and believe in the Lord may himself need to repent and believe in the Lord."

Many of his listeners began to squirm uncomfortably in their chairs. He continued, "Is it possible for a man to be so advanced spiritually that he is no longer winning souls? I tell you that this is something you cannot outgrow; it is a lifetime undertaking. Some of you who think you are further along spiritually have been told that it is the mark of a mature believer to be a 'channel of living water.' I do not totally disagree. We need to be joined to the Holy Spirit so that living water may flow through us.

"But let me also say that the channel of life has two ends: One end is open toward the Holy Spirit; but the other end is open toward men. The water of life will not flow if only the end toward the Lord is open. The other end, the end toward the world must be open too for there to be any flowing. The reason many do not have power before God is due to their either being closed on the end toward the Lord or on the end toward sinners. China can still be won to Christ if we open our hearts to men."

"But we are so few, and our country is so large. You have given us an impossible task," said one of the coworkers.

"I have given you nothing," responded Watchman. "It is the Lord who gives. And it is His task to perform through you. Besides," he added, "I have made some calculations that should encourage you: If each of us in this room leads one person to Christ in the next half year and we disciple that person for the entire six months, then at the end of that time both we and our discipled friend win one person apiece and train him for another six months, and so on, we would not only win China to Christ within a generation, but the entire population of the world will have been reached! It is simple geometric progression."

"It is simply God's will," chimed in John Wang.

"Tell us the story of Commander Deeds," shouted a friend of Watchman's near the back of the room.

"Yes, it is time for everyone to know that story," whispered Ruth Lee, seated near Watchman's podium.

"Beloved," he began, "what I tell you now truly happened. A young man named Todd was led to Christ by a wise couple from a church in his neighborhood. He had been a rebellious youth, but on the day that he was saved, he asked the couple what he should do to show his obedience to the Lord. Over tea in their home, they told him that the gospel would never make inroads in their town until a certain battalion commander was converted.

"Young Todd asked who this Commander Deeds

was. They said that he was a retired military man over sixty years of age who thought all Christians were hypocrites and who cursed and beat any Christian who dared to preach the gospel to him or even to pass by his house. He kept a pistol at home and threatened to open fire on anyone who preached to him. Having heard this, Todd immediately prayed, 'O Lord, You have shown grace to me. This is the first day of my salvation. I will go and witness to him.' Before tea was finished, and less than two hours after his own salvation, he was on his way to the commander's house.

"Fearing for his life, the couple begged him not to go. The commander's anger grew fiercer by the day, they told him, but Todd would not change his mind. He arrived at the house and knocked on the door. The commander answered with a rod in his hand and snarled, 'What do you want, boy?' Todd asked if he could come in and for some reason the hostile man allowed him entrance.

"The boy wasted no words. 'I pray that you will accept the Lord Jesus as your Savior!' he blurted out. The commander raised his rod in the air to intimidate the youth, then shouted, 'I suppose you're new around here, so this time I will pardon you; no one talks to me about Jesus, but this time I will not beat you. Now consider yourself fortunate and get out of here quickly!'

"Though he knew his life was in danger, Todd refused to leave. 'I beg you to believe on the Lord Jesus,' he said. The commander was furious. He went upstairs and came down with his pistol. 'Go, or I will shoot you now,' he threatened. Todd answered, 'I have come to ask you to believe in the Lord Jesus. If you want to shoot me, go ahead. But before you do, let me pray for you.' He knelt before the commander and prayed, 'O God, here is a man who does not know You. Please save him!' He stayed on his knees while the commander towered over him with the gun. 'Have mercy on him, Lord!' he cried out. 'Have mercy on the commander.'

"Young Todd prayed like this for several minutes before he heard a sigh, then the sound of the pistol being laid aside. Soon the commander knelt down beside him and, after a moment of weeping, prayed, 'O God, have mercy on Commander Deeds.'

"The commander was saved at that instant, and after praying some more, he rose and took the hand of his young friend, saying, 'I have heard the gospel all my life, but today I have seen the gospel for the first time.' On the following Lord's Day, Commander Deeds went to the church to worship. And before he died, he led several dozen people to the Lord."

Every eye in the auditorium was on Watchman; the audience was deeply moved by his story. "Beloved," he said, "there are two big days in the life of the believer: the day on which he believes in the Lord—and every day after that when he leads someone to faith in Christ. This is my challenge to you. Witness to at least one person a day. Witness to whomever you meet.

"It is useless for the gospel to be preached only from the pulpit. Many can preach but cannot win souls. If you bring people to them who need the Lord, they are out of their depth. Learn this truth: Only those who know how to deal with souls and lead them to Christ are useful to the church. It is time for us to put feet to our faith."

Days later, Watchman modeled his message by leaving on a dangerous mission to evangelize the remote southwestern provinces of China. He chose as his traveling companion one of his few friends who owned a car, a recently converted businessman called Shepherd Ma, who had more zeal than knowledge when it came to driving. They packed the Model T Ford with full gasoline cans and donated Bibles and set off down the brand-new motor road.

In addition to the risk of encountering Communist troops, their limited driving skills afforded them as much adventure as they needed. On more than one unfenced hairpin curve through the mountains above Kweichow, Watchman's heart almost failed him when Shepherd, squinting behind thick-lensed glasses and brimming with the overconfidence of a nearsighted driver, steered the car toward a precipitous cliff. As inexperienced as he was, Watchman began to grow accustomed to grabbing the wheel away to save their lives.

When they first passed through the mountains and drove down into the villages, their fame preceded them everywhere they went—but not for the reason they had hoped. Initially, the crowds gathered not because of their interest in hearing the gospel, but in order to see this remarkable vehicle that brought the first long-distance travelers ever to negotiate their mountain passes. Watchman and Shepherd saw their opportunity, however, and preached the Good News of Christ to everyone they met.

In this manner, the gospel spread throughout the provinces, and Watchman and Shepherd had hours in the car to discuss how to lead people to Christ.

"I am learning much from our journey together, Brother Ma," said Watchman, as the Model T chugged through the Yunnan Province.

"What is that, dear To-sheng?" asked Shepherd, always anxious to hear what God was teaching his companion.

"I am learning that impressing upon believers the importance of witnessing is not the same thing as teaching them how to lead people to the Lord—and the lack of such knowledge will render most of their witnessing ineffective."

"I am realizing the 'how' from watching you these several weeks," replied Shepherd.

"And what are your perceptions, my friend?" asked Watchman.

"That you always prepare your heart first before the Father before you try to lead anyone to His Son."

"You are exactly right, Shepherd. Prayer is the basic work of saving souls. Before you speak to a person, you must first pray to God. I once knew two brothers who were very zealous in leading men to the Lord. But in my contact with them, I knew instantly that something was wrong. They did not pray for those whom they wished to win to Christ. An interest in men void of a burden before God is simply inadequate and is therefore ineffective. One must first have a burden before God and then labor among men."[1]

"But there are times when I pray fervently and still see no results," said Shepherd.

"Perhaps it is a matter of God's timing, my friend. Some fruit take longer to ripen than others. It is just as wrong to pick an unripened apple as it is never to go into the orchard at all. Or your problem could be a deeper one," said Watchman.

"What do you mean, To-sheng? You can speak to me bluntly."

"I will seldom be as invasive with you as God is with me, Shepherd, but perhaps the problem is unconfessed sin in your own life. He said through the prophet, 'Behold, the Lord's hand is not shortened, that it cannot save; neither is his ear heavy, that it cannot hear; but your iniquities have separated between you and your God, and your sins have hid his face from you, so that he will not hear' (Isaiah 59:1-2).

"God's love is the greatest force in the world. Nothing can stand against it except sin. 'If I regard iniquity in my heart,' said King David, 'the Lord will not hear' (Psalm 66:18). Brother Paul told young Timothy to hold 'on to faith and a good conscience;

some have rejected these and so have shipwrecked their faith' (1 Timothy 1:19). So you see that faith is the cargo and your conscience is the ship. If the ship is wrecked, the cargo will fall out. When your conscience is strong, your faith is secure; but when your conscience accuses you of sin, your faith will leak out. Understand this then: When there is no unconfessed sin between you and God, then your prayers for the lost will be heard and your witnessing will be effective."

"As usual, Brother Nee, you have a way of making me understand my own poor heart. But when all of these things are in order, I still have difficulty leading people to Christ."

Watchman thought for a moment, then told Shepherd, "If your heart is right before God, then ask Him to break your heart for the souls of men. I heard of a man in England, named Dr. Chalmers, who became one of the greatest evangelists of his day soon after the following experience. He'd been invited for dinner at a home where a highly educated, well-positioned agnostic was also present. They immediately took to one another and followed their delightful dinner conversation with a lengthy discussion of world affairs. Fondly bidding one another goodnight, they retired to adjacent bedrooms.

"Just minutes later, Dr. Chalmers heard a sound like something heavy falling in the next room. He ran over and discovered his new friend's dead body on the floor. As other guests gathered in the room of the deceased, Dr. Chalmers stood and said, 'Had I known that this would happen, I would not have spent the past two hours chatting about so many things. I would have pointed him to eternal things. But, alas, I have not used even five minutes to speak to him of the salvation of his soul. I did not even give him a chance. If I had known then what I know now, I would have used all my strength to tell him how Jesus was crucified on the cross for him. But now it is too late. Had I spoken those words to him at that time, you all might have laughed at me and considered my conversation as inappropriate. Though I now say these words, the time is too late. At supper I could have said them, words which now I hope you all will listen to. Each and every one of you needs the Lord Jesus and His cross. Let me tell you, separation from God is eternal, not temporary.'

"How sad that it took a tragedy to awaken in Dr. Chalmers a spiritual sensitivity to those around him. My dear Shepherd, when God has broken both of our hearts for those we are about to encounter, they will know it immediately, and His love can win them yet."

When Watchman returned from this adventure with Shepherd Ma in time for the third annual teaching conference, he received two wonderful messages. The first was that new churches connected to the Little Flock movement were springing up all over the area—partly due to the increased missionary zeal of the believers in Shanghai. As he had known instinctively for some time, the local church could be the only valid center from which China would be won to Christ.

The second piece of news was of a more personal nature and captured Watchman's emotional interest immediately. His childhood friend and sweetheart, Charity Chang, was now in Shanghai, having earned her M.A. in English at Yenching University. He faced a dilemma: Should he contact her, or should he keep his ten-year-old vow to save his heart for the Lord and give it to no woman?

eleven

Watchman had discreetly followed Charity's school career from afar, and the last he knew she still cared little for spiritual things. But the message he now received from one of his friends was that she had been attending Bible studies, was seeking baptism, and confessed a complete spiritual transformation. Still, secondhand information is often inaccurate, and he knew that he must see her face to face. *One look into her eyes and I will know,* he thought.

The next week he arranged to meet with her after a church service. Listening to her talk about her love for the Lord and seeing that she was no longer the worldly girl he had known (although still strikingly beautiful), Watchman was shaken to the core. He immediately went back to his house to spend time alone with God in prayer.

"Father," he cried out, "what shall I do? I have promised that I would desire nothing on this earth besides You. Is it possible that after all these years I still care for her? Help me to put her out of my mind or give me faith to believe that this is from You."

God's choice was to give him faith: Faith Chang, that is, who appeared at Watchman's door on a match-making mission. Out of breath, she said, "To-sheng, now that my sister Charity has become an earnest Christian, serving the Lord with steadfast purpose, would you consider marriage with her? I feel sure she would have no objections."[1]

Watchman believed that he had heard from God, and to his delight, Charity accepted his proposal. But there was much opposition to the marriage from both sides of the family. Many who looked up to Watchman as a hero of faith were scandalized to think that he, a godly man intent on holiness, would compromise himself by giving unworthy attention to sex and raising a family. They feared that Charity's physical beauty would distract him from spiritual pursuits. On the other side stood Charity's mean-spirited aunt, Mei-chen, who broadcast that the eldest Nee son, a controversial preacher and notoriously poor, was a terrible match for her brilliant niece, Charity.

The young couple would not be deterred. Mei-chen sent a note to Watchman, demanding that he pay her the customary courtesy call. She added that if he did not, she would make big trouble for him. Perhaps she wanted to berate him to his face or force him to beg her permission to marry Charity. But his own integrity would not allow him to be cowed by her threats. To her exasperation, he gave little regard to her efforts to intimidate him, and the wedding went ahead as scheduled.

On the afternoon of October 19, 1934, the anniversary of his parents' wedding thirty-five years earlier, Watchman and Charity were united in holy matrimony after a Bible conference at Hangchow, the ancient capital known for its romantic setting. His best man was Witness Lee, a young coworker from Chefoo whom he had befriended and recently invited to join the ministry in Shanghai.

All seemed right as they exchanged vows in the company of more than four hundred believers and later sat down to a sumptuous feast with their dearest friends. Little did they know, however, that back in Shanghai, Charity's aunt was hatching a plot that would threaten to destroy the newlyweds' joy.

Mei-chen exacted her revenge by purchasing space for a week in a national daily newspaper to print a vitriolic attack on Watchman's character. Upon their return from Hangchow and for the six days following, Watchman and Charity suffered silently while their countrymen read the same polemic published repeatedly. In a less litigious day, when lawsuits were a rarity, Mei-chen gave full vent to her brooding hostility, accusing Watchman of shady dealings with foreign investors, gross misrepresentation of himself to her niece, and immoral conduct in his ministry. She even went so far as to print thousands of handbills with the same message and had them distributed in all the Christian circles. Of course, the bridegroom's enemies, most of whom were envious of his growing influence as a churchman, were only too happy to pass the article along. After reading the libelous piece, one missionary said, "The article I read was so vile that I burnt it and then felt I needed a bath." [2]

Watchman was devastated. He took to his bedroom and refused to see anyone but Charity. One day, she came in and asked him, "What will you do, my love? You have been publicly maligned and your friends await your response."

"My response is not to respond," he answered. "The second wisest man on earth said, 'If a man's ways are pleasing to the Lord, He will make even his enemies to be at peace with him' (Proverbs 16:7). But I must tell you, dear one," he said behind tear-swollen eyes, "I cannot pretend that this doesn't hurt." At that came a knock on the door.

"I'll send them away," said Charity, adding, "as I have all the others." But this female visitor was a resolute missionary friend who had attended many of the meetings at Hardoon Road.

"He'll see me," she boldly announced, "because I have a message for him from God." With her Bible in hand, she marched past Charity and right into his room, declaring, "No weapon that is formed against you shall prosper; and every tongue that rises up in judgment you shall condemn" (Isaiah 54:17).

Soon after the friend left, Charity's sister, Faith, came calling. She reminded Watchman that his gains far exceeded his losses. "Does it really matter what they say?" she gently chided him. "You have won a wife after your own heart!"[3]

Of this time in his life, Watchman later wrote, "This surely is a time of temptations; everything is confusing, cold, and harsh. In this hour it is indeed difficult for Christians to stand. But have we not known this from the beginning? What else can we say? We walk in solitude and bewilderment; we must either put down our weapons or be raptured. O Lord, which do You think is best?"[4]

Eventually the support of his friends and the tender ministry of his inner being by the Holy Spirit brought Watchman out of his depression—and not a day too soon. Word arrived from the separatist London Group of Brethren that Watchman was being charged with "compromising the fellowship." This came after they discovered that, during his visit to their country, Watchman had taken communion with lesser British Christians who held that "anyone claiming to be a believer was allowed to break bread without regard to the religious and other associations in which he was involved." The London Group's purpose for writing now was to "enlighten the Shanghai Brethren as to the true principles of Christian fellowship and to help them to judge Nee's actions."[5]

The communication from England further informed the church in Shanghai that if they wanted to remain associated with the London Group of Brethren, they must cut all connections with other groups and the missionary congregations in particular. "We have the truth on this matter," they claimed, "and you are obligated to the Lord to embrace it, profit by it, and stand firmly by it."

The church elders gathered with Watchman to discuss the problem. John Sung asked, "Pastor Nee, what are they referring to when they write that you have 'compromised the fellowship'?"

"You already know the answer to that," said Watchman matter-of-factly, "for all of you here know that, when in England, I worshipped with the beloved minister T. Austin-Sparks at the Christian Fellowship Center in Honor Oak Road, South London."

"But they are not apostate," offered Faithful Luke. "They represent one of the finest evangelical churches in Great Britain."

"Precisely," replied Watchman. "In fact, it is my opinion that they have much to teach both us and the London Group of Brethren."

"That is dangerous talk," said Y. A. Wu, always the cautious one. "Let us not forget our official association with the Brethren and that they were the first to recognize the validity of our church."

"My dear brother Wu," answered Watchman, "better that we are recognized by the Holy Spirit, in whom we were 'all baptized into one body, whether Jews or Greeks, whether bond or free; and were all made to drink of one Spirit.' If He was right when He said through the apostle Paul that we 'all are one in Christ Jesus,' then, as New Testament believers, we have a decision to make."

"What decision is that?" asked Witness Lee.

"Whether we care more what the world thinks of us than we do of God's opinion of our faithfulness. The world pays great attention to personal status—to what race I belong, what background I have, and so forth. 'I must maintain my honor,' it says. 'I must protect my status.' But once we become Christians, we should exclude all such discriminations. No one should bring his personal status or position into Christ and the church—the one new man; to do so would be to bring in the old man. Nothing that belongs to the old man should ever be carried over into the church."

"Whether we choose to recognize it or not, Brother Nee," said John Sung, "there will always be differences between nations. What of the English who look down on our ministry even now, or our neighbors, the Japanese, who threaten our very security? Perhaps it is time for us to learn to discern our enemies from our friends."

"Aside from Satan, the Lord has no enemies," replied Watchman, "only potential friends. And these differences you speak of are cultural, not spiritual. No matter what language our neighbors speak, the Holy Spirit speaks but one: the language of love. It is a good thing that some of us were not on the Jerusalem Council in Acts 15, or we might have passed a law that all Gentiles must first become Jews before they can become Christians!"

Watchman looked around the circle of church elders and said gently, "No, my friends. There are no longer any national distinctions. Every time we come to the Lord, we come not as English or Chinese but as Christians. We can never approach the Lord on the basis of our nationality. These outside things must be shut out, for we are united by the life of Christ. Whether some are American, English, Indian, Japanese, or Chinese believers, we are all brothers and sisters in the Lord. No one can divide us as God's children. We cannot have American Christianity; if we insist on having America, we cannot have Christ. The same is true of us in China. If we put our nationalism before our faith, we cannot have Christ.

"A story that I heard illustrates this well. After the war, some brothers from England went to Germany to attend a Christian conference. One of the brothers in Germany arose to introduce the visitors by saying, 'Now that the war is over, we have some English brothers visiting us to whom we extend our warmest welcome.' Among those thus introduced, one stood up and replied, 'We are not English brothers, but brothers from England.' How well spoken were those words! In Christ, we are all brothers and sisters."[6]

"Ah, but you yourself have taught us that there are distinctions between brothers and sisters," broke in Y. A. Wu. "Does not Holy Scripture say that a woman should not be permitted to teach or have authority over a man?"

"Again you are speaking culturally and not spiritually," responded Watchman. "When the church meets, the man functions differently from the woman, just as in the family, husband and wife hold different responsibilities. And who is to say whether the husband's or the wife's responsibilities are the more important? A strong case could be made for both. But in Christ, there can be no male and female. Neither the man nor the woman has any peculiar position. Why? Because Christ is all and is in all. In the spiritual life there is no way to differentiate between male and female.

"Brother Lee," said Watchman, turning to Witness Lee. "Do you remember what our carpenter friend said when I asked him, 'Daniel, what is the spiritual condition of the brothers in your place?' "

"I will never forget," answered Witness. "He said, 'Are you asking about the male brothers or the female brothers?' "

At that, all of the men had a good laugh, and Watchman continued, "Exactly! I considered that an excellent expression. He did not know whether I meant the brothers or the sisters. In Christ there is no disparity. Therefore, let new believers take to heart that when we come to Christ, we have transcended the relationship of male and female.

"We are all brothers and sisters. We are each a new creation in Christ. All natural distinctions have been annulled in Christ. We therefore must shut out of our hearts any divisive spirit. There is only one answer that the Spirit of Christ will allow us to give to the Brethren in London. Are we all in agreement on this?"

The Shanghai elders were unanimous in their response that summer to the London Group. Their reply, a courteous and scripturally based appeal to their sponsors in England, showed how far their understanding of the New Testament church had come in the few years that China had been open to the gospel. They wrote:

> We must distinguish between "sins" (either morally or doctrinally) that hinder fellowship with God and "sins" which do not. We know definitely that sins like adultery and disbelief in Christ coming in the flesh would certainly put one out of fellowship, but as to the other "sins," say that of "bad association," fellowship with God is not hindered.
>
> The fact remains that many a child of God in the different systems whom we have thought unfit for fellowship, is having a closer walk with God and a richer communion with the Lord than we.
>
> It is the Spirit, and the Spirit alone, who can decide the question of one's fitness for fellowship.
>
> The reason we receive a man is that God has received him (Romans 14:3). So the

> *divine command is, "Now him that is weak in faith, receive" (Romans 14:1). We must receive those whom God had received. This command is clear, decisive and embracing.*

The Shanghai brothers had high hopes that their English colleagues would recognize the biblical rationale for their decision and be moved to reconciliation. The very opposite reaction was forthcoming. A letter postmarked August 31, 1935, arrived in the autumn with a scathing rebuke of Watchman's leadership and a denunciation of the Chinese church—even going so far as to doubt the sincerity of their love for Christ.

In withdrawing the London Group's support of the Little Flock movement, the letter stated, "We grievously failed in our lack of holy care in laying hands too quickly on those with whom we were insufficiently acquainted. We are unable to walk with you. This, of course, applies also to all those maintaining links of fellowship with you."[7]

The Shanghai church was deeply shocked and saddened by the negative response. Watchman's grief was multiplied when he saw that the letter was signed by his old friend, Charles Barlow. At that moment, the words of the messianic passage in Zechariah 13:6 came to him: "If someone asks *the prophet,* 'What are these wounds on your body?' he will answer, 'The wounds I was given at the house of my friends.' "

twelve

While the decision of the London Group was to build a fence around their fellowship and entrench themselves in exclusivism, the Little Flock movement chose to tear down those fences and spread the gospel even beyond the borders of China. Watchman and several of his coworkers crossed the River of Golden Sand into Tibet and found a warm reception among the villagers. When many of them found salvation in Christ, the company faced the task of translating portions of Scripture into the Tibetan language and training leaders to start indigenous churches.

In a similar manner, other evangelistic teams from Shanghai continued to go out, and soon there were more than thirty new churches representing the movement throughout the country. The way they began was simple. After winning several locals to Christ, the evangelists centered their missionary activity in a believer's home, all the while feeding the converts with transcriptions of Watchman's sermons and articles from his magazine. His gift for explaining doctrines in straightforward, understandable terms gave each of the house churches a strong foundation on which to build.

That the establishment of these local churches became the goal of his entire ministry was apparent in the introduction of a book he wrote during these years of outreach, *The Assembly of Life:*

"Before time eternal," he wrote,

> *God had a will and a foreordained plan of His own. His goal is to have a group of people containing His life who are like His Son. The goal of God was to establish the church. Unfortunately, many believers fail to emphasize this. Instead, they replace the church of God with various kinds of works. There are some who establish missions, encourage foreign evangelism, zealously donate money, and form national councils. If these good things replace the church, then we are definitely deceived by Satan. I say strongly that unless our aim, work, and living today are for the church—that is, for what God is after—we are a big failure. If Sunday schools, orphanages, and humanistic societies are only for themselves, they*

*are meaningless. The death of the Lord
Jesus was for the church; the coming of the
Holy Spirit was for the church. What God
wants is the church. Personal victory over
sins, spiritual growth experiences and the
work of saving souls are only meaningful
when they build up the church. God's goal
for today is the church.*[1]

Watchman and his coworkers threw themselves
into this goal of planting churches made up of countrymen who would renounce their sins and commit all
of their lives to the Lordship of Christ. As one of the
small fellowships grew, it was given elders to direct its
ministry and nurture the little flock.

One of the reasons that these local assemblies
matured so quickly was that each believer became an
active participant—even as he or she grew daily in
their knowledge of the Word by studying Watchman's
Bible-centered booklets. He agreed with Luther that
the traditional separation between clergy and laity was
inspired by Satan and that the priesthood of all believers was the true *modus operandi* for the church.

He taught that the clergy-laity system with its hier-
archy, rank, and position was unscriptural and reduced
Christianity to a form of human organization. As it had
corrupted the Lord's original plan for His body, the
Western church model, with its sophisticated array of
salaried clergy, would paralyze the new believers' zeal
in China. Watchman and his colleagues determined

that there would be no distinction between clergy and laity in the Little Flock churches; all were priests together. They also understood that the real servant of God must live by faith and not be a hired employee depending on a religious organization for a salary.

Although Watchman stayed true to this belief for the remainder of his ministry, he increasingly found himself preoccupied with helping to meet the financial needs of his many coworkers (which later precipitated a real crisis in his life). In fact, by mid-1937, the movement had 128 full-time apostles out in the field, evangelizing, establishing churches, and nurturing the converts. In his heart, Pastor Nee felt responsible for all of them.

In the summer of 1937, Watchman was invited to preach the gospel in Manila. While conducting meetings there, he received news that the Japanese had launched a full-scale invasion of China, beginning with their seizure of Peking. The Japanese war machine, under the leadership of Emperor Hirohito, was encouraged by Hitler and Mussolini's early successes in Europe and Africa.

The civil war between Chiang Kai-shek's Nationalist Party and Mao Tse-tung's Communist Party was temporarily put on hold when, on August 14, Japanese warplanes bombed Chinese cities. Highly disciplined and well-equipped troops overran eastern China. The brutality and killing that characterized their sacking of the former Nationalist capital became known as the "rape of Nanking." The Japanese juggernaut then turned its attention toward Shanghai.

Watchman knew that he had little time to rescue his beloved Charity. To the sound of Chinese war-planes making reprisal attacks on Japanese shipping on the Whangpoo River near their home, he sneaked back into Shanghai from the south and found his wife safe with the Christian sisters at Hardoon Road church. Together they made their way through the war-ravaged streets to their home, all within earshot of the land combat just to the north. Finding the house ransacked by the invaders, they gathered what little they could carry, thinking it odd that the Chinese Bible he had presented to her at their wedding had been stolen.

Taking back roads to avoid the battle areas, the couple eventually arrived in Hong Kong, where Watchman's parents were living. While there, he was approached by some missionary friends who convinced him that this would be an opportune time for him to accompany them to England. There was a clamoring among many Christian circles in Great Britain to have his writings translated into English. After praying about it with Charity and his family, he knew he must return to London. Late that summer, unaware that his wife was pregnant, Watchman boarded an Anchor Line ship and sailed once again for England.

Upon arrival, he joined up with his friend T. Austin-Sparks of the Christian Fellowship Center at Honor Oak Road. They traveled south together to the annual Deepening of the Spiritual Life convention in Keswick. The conference was being chaired by W. H. Aldis, the venerable home director of the China Inland Mission, one of the few missionary associations for which Watchman had high esteem. Earlier in his life he had come under the influence of CIM's legendary founder, J. Hudson Taylor, from whom he had learned much about the matter of abiding in Christ.

W. H. Aldis invited Watchman to pray for the conference and inadvertently seated him next to another guest speaker who happened to be from Japan. As he crossed the platform to lead the audience in prayer, the Chinese pastor, freshly exiled from his own war-torn city, passed the Japanese participant. As Watchman began his prayer, everyone in the crowd was aware of the tension in the air. And no one in attendance would ever forget what they heard:

The Lord reigns, he prayed. *We affirm it boldly. Our Lord Jesus Christ is reigning, and He is Lord of all; nothing can touch his authority. It is spiritual forces that are out to destroy His interests in China and Japan. Therefore, we do not pray for China; we do not pray for Japan; but we pray for the interests of Thy Son in China and Japan. We do not blame any men, for they are only tools in the hand of Thine enemy. We stand for Thy will. Shatter, O Lord, the kingdom of*

darkness, for the persecutions of The
Church are wounding Thee. Amen. [2]

A communion service closed the program that day. Under a conference banner that read "All One in Christ Jesus," Watchman shared the bread and the cup with his new Christian brother from Japan. More than one Englishman in attendance witnessed first-hand that Watchman Nee lived up to the spirit of the letter he had written to the London Group three years earlier.

He made the Christian Fellowship Center a temporary headquarters for his teaching and writing ministries, planning to return to Charity in Hong Kong after four months of work. It was there at Honor Oak Road that Watchman met Angus Kinnear, an aspiring author and missionary recruit, who later would write an excellent biography of the humble Chinese pastor, entitled *Against the Tide.* [3] Young Kinnear, who was deeply moved by the weeks he spent with Watchman, later wrote:

He was so easy to talk with, and his
Eastern cultural background made discus-
sion of our common heritage in Christ so
stimulating. When he spoke in public,
whether taking morning prayers or address-
ing a church meeting, his excellent English
conspired with the charm of his mannerisms
to make him a joy to listen to. But it was the

content of his addresses that won us. He wasted no words, but brought us straight to grips with some problem of Christian living that we had sidestepped, for on too many matters we Christians excel at "dodging the issue." He displayed too the Chinese thinker's great care in his choice of terms and often gave back new meaning to our worn evangelical clichés.

But the quality in Watchman that seemed to move Kinnear most was his penetrating insight into the spiritual motives of those around him. He continued,

Moreover he could see through us, and seeing, still be faithful. This was because always his object was to exalt the Christ he loved. Within a month of coming among us, skillfully, but with obvious concern, he put his finger right on our danger point, and that, sure enough, was our spiritual pride. God had shown him from experience, he told us gently, that "Judge not, that ye be not judged," is as surely a principle of His dealings as "Give, and it shall be given to you." No wonder, then, that notes of his talks to us have seemed, thirty years later, to leap from the tattered notebook with fresh and startling relevance.[4]

Angus Kinnear was so impressed by the Shanghai pastor that, along with his missionary activities in Asia, he devoted much of the rest of his life to turning Watchman's sermons, lectures, and conference addresses into books that would edify believers around the world.

In the meantime, Europe was teetering on the edge of another world war. From his vantage point in London, Watchman observed how the timidity of the United States and other Western democracies infused Hitler with the confidence to carry out his thinly veiled plan to conquer the world. In the face of the democracies' hesitancy to get involved, Germany, Italy, and Japan formed what became known as the Rome-Berlin-Tokyo Axis. The three nations agreed not to interfere with one another's plans for expansion. As Japan continued to commit terrible atrocities in China, Hitler's Third Reich annexed Czechoslovakia.

Watchman listened to Neville Chamberlain's infamous "peace for our time" speech when the British prime minister returned from Munich in October 1938—and knew better. As Hirohito had insidiously dug his claws into China, so Hitler would not stop with the Czechs' surrender.

As outsider in England, Watchman had a prescient sense that the end of the world was nearing. He took this time to pray and refine his teaching on the Second Coming of Christ. And then a part of his own world did end, when he received a letter from Charity in Hong Kong. She revealed her pregnancy and bravely informed her husband that she had just suffered a miscarriage of the child.

Watchman had no way of knowing that this was the only time his beloved wife would ever conceive. All that he could think of was her suffering without him halfway around the world. But with the escalation of the Sino-Japanese war, he was forced to stay in Europe more than four months longer than he had planned.

While Peace Nee cared for Charity and took her on a journey to visit the evacuated Christians in the Yunnan Province, Watchman threw himself into completing and then translating his book *Rethinking the Work*. He joined in this project with an English missionary friend named Elizabeth Fischbacher, who years earlier in China had helped him formulate his doctrine of the Holy Spirit. Now they worked intently on producing a work for English readers that would help in the ministry of the local church.

The church in England and the plethora of missionary organizations that sprung from it were woefully lacking in the area of discipleship. Some of the agencies were experiencing success in evangelism but scarcely had a clue about what to do for the converts. *Rethinking the Work* was a timely resource for the churchmen of Great Britain.

With characteristic straightforwardness and ease of expression, Watchman wrote the book to examine from Scripture God's guidelines for church life. Its publication was a breath of fresh air for a large number of Christian laborers and gave them hope that forming "fresh, living churches" was the only way to conserve the results of their labors. In May 1939, just as Watchman was about to leave England to return to Charity, *Rethinking the Work* appeared in London to rave reviews from the church. For a man who disdained popularity, he would now find it more difficult than ever to remain anonymous in his homeland.

thirteen

J apan expected to conquer China within a few years. But in 1939, while the two Asian nations were locked in deadly combat, World War II broke out in Europe. By the middle of the summer, Watchman knew that he must return home no matter what the danger. His original plan was to visit the United States and travel from there directly to China. But word reached him that the Japanese had seized many Pacific ports of entry. They waited there for any Chinese returning from the West and used "compulsory inoculations" to terminate their enemies. Watchman wisely took a British ship to India and finally arrived in Shanghai safely by way of Bombay.

Charity was there to meet him, and their reunion was a joyous experience. Watchman took Solomon seriously when he advised, "Rejoice in the wife of your youth" (Proverbs 5:18). They were very much in love, a fact obvious to everyone who knew them. Even though later in life he was scandalized by the false accusations of a Communist tribunal, Watchman knew in his heart that his life still lined up with the biblical command, "Keep the marriage bed undefiled" (Hebrews 13:4).

It was good to be home with Charity, but Shanghai hardly resembled the high-spirited, commercial city that he had left. The marketplaces were in ruins and the streets infested with beggars. A mere shadow of commerce remained, and that only because of the presence of the American, British, and French warships anchored in Whangpoo Harbor. Watchman, clad in a drab gown and a battered, old felt hat, took to roaming the alleys of Shanghai, searching for the lost and lonely. It was not unusual to find him on a rainy day, squatting under the eaves of a rundown shop, laughing and talking with a ragged assortment of the lowliest coolies. He often waited for them to finish their gambling before he provided wonton soup and preached the gospel of Christ to them.

During this time, he wrote a note to a friend,

"I have found many have already been hardened to protect themselves. And some of the better-off believers have been praising the Lord because they're not feeling anything of the sufferings around them. As for myself, I must confess I am feeling every bit of them; only I am holding onto the Lord."

Having ministered throughout the ravaged communities of this once-proud city now occupied by a foreign army, Watchman added, "What has been happening around us is enough, even if one has a thousand hearts, to break every one of them. But, my Father is God! I have never learned to love the word 'God' as much as today. God!"[1]

In Watchman's absence, the church on Hardoon Road had remained strong, mainly because of the preaching of John Chang and Dr. C. H. Yu, a practicing optometrist with a gift for Bible exposition. Upon his return, Watchman humbly stepped back into the role of leader. In light of a world at war, one of his first duties was to call the church to prayer.

On the Sunday morning after German forces stormed into Poland, Watchman taught his people about a weapon for which there was no defense. "Prayer," he said, "can do anything that God can do. Each of you is going to need to believe that more now than you ever have before. The situation in Europe will only get worse, and our own country is being torn from us. But the weapons that we must fight back with are not the weapons of the world. 'On the contrary,' " he quoted Paul, " 'they have divine power to demolish strongholds.' We must learn to be a people of prayer."

He turned to his faithful friend and asked, "Brother Yu, what has the Lord taught you about prayer?"

The diminutive eye doctor stood and replied, "That I must be more specific in my prayer life. I used to pray to God for hours and when I finished, I think He would ask Himself, 'Now I wonder what that little man wanted?' " The congregation laughed.

The good doctor continued, " 'Knock and it shall be opened unto you,' says the Lord. But I had been knocking on the wall. The Lord will not open the wall for you, because He doesn't know what you really want. 'You have not, because you ask not,' God tells us. Asking needs to be specific. This is what both seeking and knocking signify. It is seeking for one particular object; it is knocking on the door, not the wall. I am no longer satisfied with praying out of a sense of duty or simply to be in God's presence." As he seated himself again, Dr. Yu added, "I am learning to pray so that I will be heard!"

"Exactly!" exclaimed Watchman, warming to the topic with characteristic zeal. "We must learn to pray specifically. Indefinite prayers bring indefinite answers. Yet some pray with a specific object in mind and still receive no answer. Can any of you think of a reason why their prayers are not heard?"

"Of course," answered John Chang immediately. "The psalmist said, 'If I regard iniquity in my heart, the Lord will not hear my prayer' " (Psalm 66:18).

"You are right, my brother," said Watchman. But who is this man who regards iniquity in his heart? He is not the man in Romans 7 who does something that he hates. He has failed but he hates that failure, has a godly sorrow that it occurred, and resolves not to go that way again. But the man who regards iniquity in his heart is the one who will not give up his sin,

135

neither in his conduct nor in his heart. He is only sorry when he gets caught. Because the Lord is holy, He will not hear the prayer of such a person.

"Solomon said, 'He that covers his sins shall not prosper; but whoever confesses and forsakes them shall obtain mercy' (Proverbs 28:13). Sin must be confessed. After it is confessed, the Lord will forgive and forget. You should go to the Lord saying, 'Here is a sin which my heart finds hard to give up, but now I ask for Your forgiveness. I am willing to forsake it; I ask you to deliver me from it that it may not remain with me. I do not want it and I resist it.' The Lord will pass over your sin if you confess it to Him."[2]

"But, Pastor, what if I have done all these things and still receive no answer to my prayer?" asked Peace Wang. "I have prayed daily for three years that the Japanese would be turned back from our land and that the madmen who murder to possess this world will be defeated. But the only thing keeping them from controlling Shanghai completely are a few foreign ships in our harbor, and from what you tell us of the war in Europe, the wrong side is winning. How can I believe that God answers my prayers?"

This question took Watchman somewhat by surprise, because Sister Wang, one of his dearest friends, had a heart as large as her ample body and a spirit as cheerful as a child's. Still, his answer came quickly.

"Is a prayer of three years any less pressing to God if the need is still there? Our Lord said we

Watchman Nee

'ought always to pray, and not to faint' (Luke 18:1). The reason the widow in Luke 18 continued to knock is that the door continued to stay closed. But her persistence eventually opened it. We must keep on praying till the Lord is worn out, as it were, by our continual coming. This is not a sign of unbelief; rather it is just another kind of faith.

"But, our beloved sister Wang, the subject you have brought up is exactly why I have called all of you here today. How should we pray about this war? I speak to you now not as Chinese but as men and women in Christ." Watchman proceeded to rehearse for his listeners a brief but brilliant history of how God had moved through secular governments. From King Cyrus of Persia all the way to the Spanish Armada, he showed them how God's dealings with world powers have always been in relation to His own children.

Watchman raised his arms and proclaimed, "We must know therefore *how* to pray. It must be possible for British and German, Chinese and Japanese Christians to kneel and pray together and all to say 'Amen' to what is asked. If not, there is something wrong with our prayer. We may remind God of what attitude Japan takes to Him, but we must also remind Him that in China, Christians and missionaries have too much intimacy with the corrupt State. In the last European war there was much prayer that dishonored God. Let us not fall into the same error.

"The church must stand above national questions

137

and say, 'We, here, ask for neither a Chinese nor a Japanese victory, but for whatever is of advantage to the one thing precious to You, O Lord: the testimony of Your Son.' Such prayer is not empty words. If the whole church prayed thus, the war could soon be settled God's way."[3]

The war continued to rage, but Pastor Nee never allowed his flock to view the Japanese or Axis countries as their enemies. "We wrestle not against flesh and blood," he would remind them, "but against spiritual wickedness in high places." And the church at Hardoon Road grew as Watchman rightly divided the word of truth for them. One missionary who regularly attended their services described the church in 1940:

"On Sunday morning, crowds gather quietly at 9:30 to hear the preaching of the Word, the women sitting on one side and the men on the other, the hall being wider than it is long. On the backless benches all must sit as close as possible to make the maximum use of the space, for outside the building on three sides more people sit at the windows and the big double doors or listen to the loudspeakers, and there is even an overflow upstairs. As well as the poor, the educated and rich are here; doctors mingle with laborers, lawyers and teachers with rickshaw men and cooks. Among the modestly clad sisters are not a few modern women and girls with fashionable hairstyles and makeup, short sleeves and daringly slit dresses of tasteful silks. Children run about, dogs wander in, hawkers enter the lane, cars honk in the road outside, and the P.A. system is erratic. But each Sunday the Word of the Cross is faithfully preached. Sin and salvation, the new life in Christ and the eternal purpose of God, service, and spiritual warfare—all are expounded and nothing is held back. They are given the strongest food and the straightest challenge."[4]

Under Watchman's leadership, the work was expanding rapidly. When the Shanghai church outgrew its facility, neighboring buildings were purchased and renovated for use. His messages were always clear, practical, and full of spiritual power. His humor, warmth, and depth of insight were drawing large crowds from all over the city. Elizabeth Rademacher, a missionary friend in Shanghai during World War II, reminisced fifty years later about Watchman's ministry:

"His preaching was life-giving, and many impressions were so deeply implanted as to be unforgettable. One example is his comment on Romans 12:1-2, the passage that teaches that if we will commit ourselves to God, then we will know His will. Pastor Nee taught that 'God's will is not for those who are disobedient to Him. It is a question of what sort of person I am. Am I even qualified to know His will? All good is not God's will, but God's will is always good,' he would say. And I remember him giving this word to new believers: 'Salvation without commitment to the Lordship of Christ is like a railway with only one track. We need both to advance on the spiritual road.'

"One message he preached on the will of God left me overwhelmed. It portrayed the will of God from eternity past to eternity in the future. The essence of what he said was this: In the beginning there was only one will—God's undisputed will. Then Satan fell, and in the universe there was a second will—a rebellious will. Later God created man with a free will, able to choose to be one either with God or with Satan. In eternity future, after Satan has been cast into the lake of fire, there will again be only one will in the universe—but a will not the same as in the beginning, for God's will and man's will will be perfectly blended into one will."[5]

These were, perhaps, the best years that the church in Shanghai would know and Watchman and Charity's happiest in the ministry. She was always there, supporting him in every way possible, although just as humble as when it came to personal accolades. Along with her sister Faith, Peace Wang, and Ruth Lee, Charity remained in the background, heavily involved in personal counseling and meeting the needs of anyone who crossed their paths.

Meanwhile, Watchman, a soul possessed by One higher than himself, was a man in perpetual motion. Always working on his preaching craft, he filed every experience of the day away for future use as a lesson to be taught. When he wasn't at his desk poring over the Scriptures (using one of his forty methods of Bible study), he was writing magazine articles, evangelistic pamphlets, or instruction manuals for his coworkers, or teaching myriad classes on the Christian lifestyle. He was in the streets modeling his own motto: "Witness to at least one person a day." Continuing in the tradition of wearing the "gospel shirts" that he and his young friends had started back in Foochow, Watchman led new converts out into the neighborhoods, giving them field training for leading their fellow townspeople to faith.

He delighted to hear a report about one of the members of his church winning a local maidservant to Christ. She lived on a lane of twelve houses and after her conversion vowed that she would not stop until every home on the block was cleaned by a believer. So she prayed that God would give her opportunity and wisdom to carry out the task. By the time the story reached Watchman, she had already successfully evangelized six other maidservants. Such stories were becoming more common every day, and the city was buzzing with talk about the goings-on at Hardoon Road.

Watchman and Charity were learning "to live in the supernatural" and were excited each day, upon awakening, to see what the Lord had in store for them. One afternoon they were invited to tea by a woman who had a surprise wrapped up for Charity. She opened the package to find her husband's old wedding gift to her: the beloved Bible that had been stolen during the Japanese invasion.

"How in the world did you ever find this?" asked Charity.

"When you hear the story, you will know that God found it for you, not me," replied the lady. She recounted how a missionary to China, who happened to be on furlough in Ireland, stopped during his message and said, "If only I had a Chinese Bible, I could explain this passage so much more clearly!" Sure enough, such a Bible was brought up to him, and, much intrigued, he asked the bearer, "How did you come by this book?"

" 'I have a friend whose son was in the British forces when the Japanese entered Shanghai. When many of the Chinese fled their homes, he joined in the ensuing looting frenzy. Entering one of the houses, he picked up this book and read, in English, this phrase on the flyleaf: 'Reading this book will keep you from sin; sin will keep you from reading this book.' For some reason, he held onto it as a memento of his tenure in China. Later, his parents gave it to me."

"The missionary opened the book and read the inscription, recognizing the Chinese names that he translated as, 'Charity from Watchman.' " With a cup of tea in one hand and the Bible in the other, the lady kindly held the precious book out to Charity and said, "Now, by God's grace, I am able to return your wedding present to you." Charity and Watchman were deeply moved.

fourteen

There is a Chinese proverb that Watchman came to understand: "He who raises his head above the heads of others will sooner or later be decapitated." The Little Flock movement in general, and the Shanghai church in particular, made vocal enemies as they grew. Watchman was charged with shallowness because he kept the church's schedule so flexible and often followed the Spirit's moving for programming their meetings. He was accused by other Christian groups of being a "sheep stealer," because so many Chinese and missionaries were leaving their organizations to become a part of his ministry.

One countryman, who claimed to have "inside information," published and distributed a pamphlet claiming that Watchman was steadily supported by large amounts of foreign capital, accusing him of misuse of those funds. To make matters worse, a missionary friend, whose envy got the better of him, turned on Watchman and wrote a widely read magazine article that unjustly lambasted both his person and his work.

When advised to defend himself, Watchman said, "If I proved myself right, my brother would be proved wrong; but what advantage would it be to me that my brother was proved wrong? No, I was warned in Scripture that 'all who would live godly in Christ Jesus shall suffer persecution' (2 Timothy 3:12). I can expect no less."[1] Still, fits of depression seized him periodically, and he had to fight through them for emotional peace. His natural bent toward optimism would serve him well during the hard times to come.

Japan had been trying to conquer China since the late 1930s. Although Japan now occupied much of eastern China, the Chinese would not surrender. So when war broke out in Europe in 1939, Japan saw the opportunity to expand elsewhere by confiscating European possessions in Southeast Asia. The United States intervened to stop Japanese aggression by banning the sale to Japan of war materiel, such as steel, iron, and oil for airplanes. As Japan began to feel the squeeze, General Tojo Hideki decided to take drastic action.

General Tojo ordered a surprise attack on the American fleet at Pearl Harbor, Hawaii. Early on Sunday, December 7, 1941, Japanese planes destroyed or damaged nineteen ships, smashing American planes on the ground and killing more than twenty-four hundred soldiers and civilians.

The next morning, a dismal, rainy day in Shanghai, the Japanese sank the American and British gunboats in Whangpoo Harbor and made a lightning-quick strike on Shanghai's five million citizens. Angus Kinnear wrote of that day:

"The action was swift and complete. Barbed wire barricades were flung across the roads, cars were commandeered, bicycles were at a premium, buses disappeared, food prices quickly soared. As the death rate increased, warehouses were piled high with coffins, because none who died in the city could be carried out for burial. Crime grew fast, and the Japanese did not care. Fear of their terrible retaliation protected them."[2]

The church lived in fear and it seemed that things could not get worse. But just a few days later they did. As the Japanese prepared to move against Hong Kong, word reached Watchman that his beloved father, Weng-shiu Nee, had died suddenly from a heart attack. Brokenhearted over his father's death and fearing for his mother's safety, Watchman secretly traveled to Hong Kong to make the funeral arrangements. This was one of the most difficult times in his life.

When he returned to the church in Shanghai, Watchman faced a financial crisis of the highest magnitude. The Japanese occupation of eastern China had brought commerce to a standstill. Support that church members had been able to give was now almost nonexistent at a time when hundreds of newly planted churches needed funding and thousands of recent converts required expensive Christian education and spiritual care. *Christianity Today* reported that by this time, the Little Flock movement embraced seventy thousand members in seven hundred congregations. Watchman was responsible for 128 full-time "apostles," itinerant ministers who were on the road starting up new churches and evangelizing wherever they went. The church in Shanghai alone boasted more than two hundred coworkers who needed support.

Some financial aid arrived from Christian friends in England, but Watchman knew that unless God brought relief from some unexpected source, the Christian movement in China was in trouble. He and Charity prayed relentlessly over the problem and, soon after, an answer came. Whether the answer came from God or not, Watchman afterwards was never quite sure. It appeared in the form of his brother, George, a research chemist with his own laboratories, who invited Watchman to become his partner in establishing a pharmaceutical company in Shanghai.

There was no way for Watchman to know that joining his brother in this commercial enterprise would eventually lead to his torture and death at the hands of Communist captors. In fact, because of his decision, Watchman began to meet one disaster after another, each one increasingly menacing. But at the time, all Watchman knew was that the opportunity that faced him was a timely one.

In the early months of 1942, the China Biological and Chemical Laboratories (CBC) was launched in Shanghai. One of China's first manufacturers of synthetic drugs, CBC employed many of Watchman's coworkers and apostles part-time, helping them to earn enough to continue their ministries during the rest of the week. As chairman of the newly formed board of directors, Watchman routinely moved back and forth between his business appointments and the work of the church.

It wasn't long before his longtime friend, Faithful Luke, and a delegation of colleagues appeared at the modest Nee home for a confrontation. Sitting in a room whose only decorations were blackout curtains and antishatter strips across the windows, Faithful Luke began: "My dear To-sheng, why have you left the work of God to go into commerce?"

"You were never one to waste words, my old friend," replied Watchman, "but I am merely doing what Brother Paul did in Corinth and Ephesus." Knowing in his heart that the continual barrage of criticism had wounded his spirit, he nevertheless added, "It is something exceptional, and it is part-time. I give an hour a day to training company representatives; after that I do the Lord's work."

Chen Zexin, one of Watchman's closest coworkers, remarked, "But when Paul made his tents, it was a simple handwork. The business you are doing is a big enterprise. It needs total commitment to run this business well. Because of that, the time left for the Lord and serving the brothers will be reduced accordingly. You must reconsider."

Watchman looked down at the floor and, with sadness in his voice, said, as much to himself as to his visitors, "I am like a woman who has lost her husband and must go out to work from financial necessity."

Inevitably, the elders of the church in Shanghai, including his confidante, Dr. Yu, labeled him as a renegade, citing the verse, "No one who puts his hand to the plow and looks back is fit for service in the kingdom of God" (Luke 9:62). Their judgment was that the one who had helped found the Hardoon Road church was now unfit to preach there. Once again, Watchman was deeply hurt, betrayed by his friends, but he quietly resolved to continue to provide financial support for the coworkers who had come to depend on him.

For their part, believers all over China and especially those in Shanghai were shaken by the decision. They did not know what to think and waited to hear his defense. But no man mentored by Margaret Barber is experienced at vindication, so characteristically he accepted the action as God's own discipline and chose silence over self-exoneration.

During this crisis, Charity overheard Watchman's end of a phone conversation with an irate colleague. Her husband patiently listened to the harangue, now and then interjecting, "Yes. . .yes. . .thank you. . . thank you."

After he hung up, Charity asked, "Whoever was that?"

"It was a brother telling me all I have been doing wrong," he answered.

"And were you guilty of all that?" she asked, knowing that he wasn't.

"No," he said softly.

Charity was infuriated by Watchman's self-righteous critics. "Then why," she exclaimed, "did you not give him an explanation instead of just saying, 'Thank you'?"

"My beloved wife," came the reply, "if anyone exalts your husband to heaven, he is still Nee To-sheng. And if anyone tramples him down to hell, he remains Nee To-sheng." Then quoting Job, he said, "Shall we accept only good from God, and not trouble also?" (Job 2:10b). As far as he was concerned, no other words were needed. God was in control.

At another time, a sympathetic young friend approached him and asked why he accepted his lot without fighting back. His reply was classic Watchman Nee:

"You will see someday that time is needed for real life to mature. Other than having a big head, youth cannot much be matured. Maturity is a matter of the enlargement of capacity. You must allow God to give you time to suffer beyond measure; then your capacity will be enlarged. Some could suffer the loss of five dollars but could never suffer the loss of five thousand dollars. Some could forgive others two or three times, but the fifth time would make their hands tremble."

"But could not one decide to act mature and by acting so long enough become the very thing he imitates?" asked the young man.

Watchman replied, "One discovers by eating whether a fruit is raw or ripe. Raw fruit tastes sour and bitter and is tough and hard. Only ripe fruit tastes sweet and fragrant. It takes time to ripen fruit and it takes hard times to mature a Christian. That is why we must never try to escape the discipline of the Holy Spirit. To escape it just one time is to lose an opportunity to have our capacity enlarged. This will prolong the time required for life to mature in us and will even require us to make up this lesson in order to reach maturity."

"Are you saying, then, that I should look forward to difficulties?" asked the youth. "You are asking too much of me."

"I am asking nothing," said Watchman. "Scripture says, 'Consider it pure joy, my brothers, whenever you face trials' (James 1:2). The fact is that you will never be the same after you pass through suffering. Either you will have your capacity enlarged or you will become more hardened. For this reason, when you are experiencing hard times, you must pay attention. I always ask my friends the same question after they have passed through suffering: 'What have you learned from the Lord?' "

The young man went home, pondering the words he had heard, while Watchman went back to his impossible situation.

Not only was he excommunicated from preaching in his own church, but his beloved friend, Ruth Lee, who had supported him from the beginning, was convinced by others to leave him, though she did so with great sadness. Chen Zexin wrote of this time,

"That was a rather dark period. Many souls were suppressed, deeply grieved. Those who loved the Lord with all their hearts could only shed tears, worry, grieve, and pray."

But Watchman Nee would not be stopped. He and George moved the factory to Chungking, where he purchased a campsite for the training of lay ministers to spur on the spiritual awakening that was still growing in the provinces not controlled by Japan. For the next three years he traveled back and forth between Shanghai and Chungking. He was both CEO of a highly successful business that gave Christian refugees and his own coworkers employment and an itinerant evangelist who cared enough about new converts to teach them how to grow in the Christian life.

Meanwhile, the Hardoon Road church suffered without Watchman's leadership. The Japanese occupation made it almost impossible to meet as usual. The foreign army set up a blockade complex of road barriers that they often engaged on a moment's notice, sometimes trapping church members in an area from which they could not return home for days or even weeks at a time. The church held an emergency meeting and decided that the only way they could continue to exist would be to divide into house churches for the time being. Watchman heard of their plight and longed to be there to help them.

The church limped along while Japan's attention turned to the West. The Axis powers were being dismantled. On islands that were once held by the Japanese, Americans built air bases to enable them to carry the war closer to Japan. By 1944, American ships were blockading Japan, while American bombers pounded Japanese cities and industries. The Allied forces were winning the day and Japan was coming to understand that her ambitions in China might never be realized.

On August 6, 1945, an American plane dropped an atomic bomb on the midsized city of Hiroshima, killing seventy thousand people. Three days later, a second atomic bomb killed more than forty thousand in Nagasaki. Emperor Hirohito forced his government to surrender to the Allies on September 2. One week later, Watchman's life was changed when Japan signed an armistice with China and began to withdraw their troops. Watchman could once again travel and continue his ministry away from Shanghai.

Knowing that he was still "exiled" from the church in Shanghai, he and Charity moved back to his boyhood home in Foochow. They reacquainted themselves with the small estate and decided that it would make a perfect training center for more church workers. They set about the work of transformation. At the same time, Watchman set in motion his own withdrawal from CBC, turning the operation over to his brother and making certain that future funds would continue to go to various ministries.

It was about this time he contacted his friend, Witness Lee, fiery preacher for the movement in Chefoo. Never forgetting about the needs of the congregation in Shanghai, Watchman knew that Witness Lee could bring enthusiasm and healing to the tense situation. He was delighted, then, to hear that Brother Lee would accept his challenge and move his family and ministry to the headquarters at Hardoon Road.

Under Witness Lee's influence, the church in Shanghai soon began to grow again. Families from the many underground "house churches" began to return to corporate worship, and renewed evangelistic efforts broke out all over the area. Still Watchman remained in the shadows, studying his Bible and writing new training manuals for saints he wasn't sure would even read them. Many believers remained confused about the rumors and innuendoes they heard regarding him. Had he actually misused church funds? Was he really guilty of collusion with the hated Japanese oppressors? Why had he chosen a secular business venture over the church? Because Watchman had never defended himself, few of them knew of his innocence in these matters.

For his part, Watchman would not budge from his

original stand. "If a man's ways are pleasing to the Lord," he quoted Solomon, "He will make even his enemies to be at peace with him" (Proverbs 16:7). With sorrow in his heart, he confided to a close friend, "I have put it in God's hands."

The main body of believers in Shanghai grew more depressed daily by the absence of their founding pastor. Finally, late in 1946, Witness Lee approached the church elders and pointedly asked them, "Were you in the Spirit when you made the decision to reject him? And what was the effect? Can you say it brought life?"[3] Their answer was a heartwrenching "no" to each of his questions. One of the coworkers confessed to Brother Lee and the whole group, "Brother Nee's case was a mortal wound to us, and words cannot tell how far the consequences go. The charge that he collaborated with the enemy is entirely groundless and much else that has been said was not based upon pure facts. This was the work of the devil and shows our own spiritual deficiency at that time, but we hope we may have learned our lesson." [4]

As it turned out, they had learned their lesson—at least for the time being. With Witness Lee as their liaison, the Shanghai elders sent a message to Watchman at Foochow, inviting him to lead a Bible conference at Hardoon Road in April. His acceptance was immediate; his joy was infectious. Not long after, he traveled to the church to find sixty coworkers from all over China, flanked by thirty elders from the Shanghai church, all waiting for him with great expectancy. After they had exchanged mutual confessions and assured one another of complete forgiveness, the reconciliation was complete. The "Number One Seat" in the row of chairs ordered by seniority was once again reserved for Watchman Nee.

When he stepped onto the platform to address the audience, an assembly hall that comfortably seated only four hundred souls was packed with more than fifteen hundred believers, "hanging from the rafters" just to hear their beloved pastor preach the Word once again.

fifteen

In March 1947, Chiang Kai-shek's Army of the Nationalist Government launched a major offensive against Mao Tse-tung and the Chinese Communist Party, which headquartered in the caves of Yenan. After capturing the city and driving Mao's forces out, the Nationalists broadcast their victory throughout the world. But it was an empty boast. The Communists were a guerrilla army and simply slipped away to poise themselves for a counterattack.

Watchman's common sense told him that even though Chiang's government was corrupt, the church was far better off under his regime than it would be after a Communist takeover. Even the Japanese occupation would have been better. He understood the consequences to Christianity if a government founded on the hostile atheism of Marxist ideology came into power. He and his friends waited and prayed.

In late June, the People's Liberation Army (PLA) swept across China to the Yangtze Valley, decimating the Nationalist troops who dared to oppose them. The Communist juggernaut was set in motion, and Pastor Nee realized the danger that was coming and the value of whatever time the church had left in China. His closest friends urged him to flee to Taiwan, but he never wavered from his original call: to penetrate all of China with the gospel of Jesus Christ. If anything, his resolve was strengthened by the crisis that surrounded him.

He called his coworkers together and revealed to them a plan that he and Witness Lee had been formulating. The two men were convinced that the way to reach their homeland for Christ was through "evangelism by migration," a concept they believed was clearly presented in the Book of Acts. Watchman explained it to his listeners: "When God scattered the people abroad through persecution, there were thousands of believers in Jerusalem and there was a constant movement outward. Yet when Paul returned to Jerusalem, there were the same large number of believers. We must not remain stationary but must move out and make room for others, for as many will be added as move out. Today, China has about 450 million inhabitants and only one million Christians. Give all Christians the same training, then send them forth, and we shall see the Church proclaiming the gospel everywhere. They need not wait for persecution. Whether by persecution or not, go forth they must."[1]

He knew that the persecution was coming but thought that God might spare them long enough to win China to Christ. "I believe," he exclaimed to his coworkers, "that within fourteen to fifteen years, the whole of China can be won with the gospel. Let us give our all for this."

His audience was deeply moved. When their pastor concluded his message with, "Render to God the things that are God's," they responded in a manner unparalleled in the Chinese church. Throughout the Little Flock churches, the phrase "Render to God. . ." brought an outpouring of sacrificial gifts from the believers. Some followed Watchman's example and signed over entire factories, businesses, and companies to the movement. It was Acts 4 all over again. Partly to show their commitment to the evangelization of China and partly to symbolize their turning away from worldly materialism, many Christians gave their jewelry, clothing, and entire life savings to the cause. The church was caught up in a mighty revival that reached all the way into believers' pocketbooks.

Soon the "gospel emigration plan" to take the whole country for Christ was set into motion. To the backdrop of civil war erupting all around them, the believers met for urgent training sessions before entire "emigrant" families would leave Shanghai and Foochow to travel inland to evangelize and plant new fellowships. Watchman and his cadre of teachers worked night and day, writing lessons and training the workers on the qualifications of a Christian servant, the ministry of God's Word, the problem of sickness, how to win souls, how to set up a church, and how to study the Bible. The sense of urgency that he communicated to the trainees magnified both the depth of commitment and the sense of excitement of the participants. He wrote an editorial in his Shanghai magazine that said, "These days are critical beyond anything we have thought." Then he went out and ministered with passion and abandon, saving nothing for a future in question.

The results were remarkable. Hundreds of families moved after their training; and by 1948, Chen Zexin reported more than two hundred new assembly halls had been established for the Kingdom. The generosity of the new converts brought uncommon financial prosperity to many of the churches (especially the church in Shanghai). The public notoriety began to draw the attention of the Communist Party, which equated the term "capitalist" with "enemy" and which was gravely suspicious of anyone who accumulated wealth.

On January 31, 1949, the People's Liberation Army marched into Peking without resistance. Less than three months later, Mao Tse-tung ordered his troops across the two-mile-wide Yangtze River. After reaching the opposite bank, the Red Army passed through nearly half a million of Chiang's Nationalists with hardly a shot being fired. When they reached the southern capital of Nanking, Watchman's worst fears were realized. China would soon be under Communist rule. His instincts told him that atheism would soon become the very air they would have to breathe.

Watchman called the believers together, and after much prayer, he felt he had an answer. The church building project in Shanghai was almost completed and soon there would be seats for four thousand worshippers. He knew that it could be many weeks before the PLA reached Shanghai, and he decided not to waste time. "There is still time to preach the gospel," he thought.

He decided to send his most trusted coworkers to fields where they might be free to minister for some time. Witness Lee would go to Taiwan, Faithful Luke to Singapore, Simon Meek to Manila, and his beloved Charity to Hong Kong.

"But what will you do?" they asked him.

"My call has not changed, dear ones," he said. "I am not much of a shepherd, but I will stay with my flock."

Witness Lee protested, "If you stay, it could be the end."

"The end of this world is the start of a better one," he answered. "And besides, remember what Peace Wang always says: 'The Lord sat as King at the Flood; He sits as King forever!'"

With a sense of things to come, Witness made one more attempt to deter his friend. "But if you don't care for your own life, then care for us who need you!"

Witness Lee's persuasion was beginning to penetrate his old friend's resolve, and struggling for words, Watchman replied passionately: "If I cared for any of you less, I would care more for my life. As it is, only one thing matters: If the house is crashing down, I have children inside and must support it, if need be with my own head."[2]

Watchman turned from Brother Lee to face the rest of his coworkers. "We must buy up the opportunities because the days are evil," he quoted Paul. "We have wasted too many chances in the past. Every day God is giving us more opportunities. To redeem the time is to seize today the opportunities God has appointed for us. When the church buries a talent, there is a serious loss. We think because our new assembly hall is completed that we can settle down for the rest of life. We preach and ten or twenty souls are saved, and we think we have done well. But if the Lord's intention was that we win a thousand souls in one day, then nine hundred souls have been lost. When God moves, let us move."[3]

And move they did. The apostles, pastors, and evangelists of the Little Flock churches redoubled their efforts; evangelism (which they sensed would be the first freedom to go) became their highest priority.

In the meantime, Mao Tse-tung was ensconced as chairman of the Chinese Communist Party with Chou En-lai as his premier. Under their leadership, the "liberating" army entered Shanghai on May 25 and the believers' lives were forever changed. One of the Communists' first actions was to close all the churches in the villages that surrounded the city. The Communists held massive rallies and held popular trials for most of the wealthy landowners and merchants. After many victims were executed, their land and holdings were taken and redistributed among the poor peasants and common laborers. It was only a matter of time before the authorities would turn their attention to the leader of the most prosperous church in Shanghai.

Chou En-lai soon set his devious plan into motion. He feared the thriving young church of China and designed a strategy to enervate it even as he made it work for his own cause. He started by calling three liberal Protestant leaders together in Peking for a late-night, closed-door meeting. There they drafted a document that Chairman Mao hoped would mark the beginning of the end of true Christianity in China.

The paper was called the *Christian Manifesto for the Protestant Churches*. It spelled out the principles of the "new Christian movement" as the premier dictated them to the three sycophantic leaders. The whole movement was to become known as the "Oppose America, Aid Korea, Three Self Reform Movement of the Church of Christ in China."

Chairman Mao's goal was to absorb the church by evacuating all foreign missionaries and making it self-governing, self-supporting, and self-propagating. Of course, offensive names like "God" and "Jesus" could no longer be used, and the only legal

Christian publication would from now on be the government periodical, *Tien Feng (Heavenly Wind)*. This eventually would mean the end of Watchman's vast publishing ministry. Time was short and he knew it.

On New Year's Day 1951, while American soldiers were fighting Communism in the rice paddies of Korea, Watchman preached one of his last recorded sermons. It was all the more remarkable because of the bleak situation he and his church were facing. He told them:

"Consider the miracle of the loaves and fishes. The point was not the quantity of materials in hand but the blessing that rested upon it. Sooner or later we must recognize that what counts is not the state of our treasury or the number of our gifts. It is from the blessing of the Lord alone that man derives his sustenance. One day our own resources, our power, our toil, our faithfulness, will all proclaim to us their meaninglessness."

Watchman looked out lovingly at his congregation, knowing that many of his listeners would soon be tested in ways they could not yet imagine. He finished his thought: "The tremendous disappointment of future days will lay bare to us our own utter inadequacy.

"This lesson, my friends, is not easily learned. The hopes of so many are still centered not on the blessing of the Lord but on the few loaves in their hands. It is so pitifully little we have in hand, and yet we keep counting on it; and the more we count on it, the harder the work becomes. My brothers and sisters, miracles issue from the blessing of the Lord!

"We should be able to trust the blessing of God and wait for it. And we will often find that, even when we have made a mess of things, somehow all is well. A little bit of blessing can carry us over a great deal of trouble.

"What is a 'blessing?' It is the working of God where there is nothing to account for His working. Many of us only expect results in keeping with our own abilities, but blessing is fruit that is out of all correspondence with what we are. It is not just the working of cause and effect, for when we reckon on the basis of what we put in, we merely bar the way for God to work beyond our reckoning. If on the other hand we set our hearts upon the blessing of the Lord, we shall find things happen that are altogether out of keeping with our capacity and that surpass even our dreams.

"Beloved," he said softly, "you must seek His blessing today. The only guarantee you can count on for tomorrow is that you will be persecuted for living a godly life in Christ Jesus." Then, one of the brightest and most gifted men in China concluded his message with, "There will come a time soon when your abilities will do nothing to save you. There will even come a time when you believe everything is finished. But with His blessing on you, that will be the beginning."

The next several months saw Communism strengthen its grip on China. Local revolutionary committees were formed in most communities, encouraging townspeople to inform on their neighbors. It seemed that the secret police were everywhere, invading the privacy of citizens and pushing the regular municipal authorities to prosecute those who were denounced as counterrevolutionaries. "Tiger hunts" were formed by party leaders to seek out and punish the capitalist tigers who "preyed" upon the wealth of the citizenry.

Then came Black Saturday, April 27, 1951, the day that thousands of Shanghai's intellectuals were arrested and turned over to a program of thought reform. Many believers were taken, among whom were some of Watchman's coworkers. Chou En-lai was building up his courage to move against China's most beloved pastor.

Five days later, *Tien Feng* published an order to the Christian church in China to participate in accusation meetings. Churches were required to publicly censure and hand over to the authorities all "imperialist elements and their stooges," and in this way prove themselves worthy to join the government's new Three Self Reform Church.

By August 11, *Tien Feng* boasted that sixty-three accusation meetings had already taken place. Each meeting was characterized by emotionally charged accusatory speeches rehearsed by the speaker to defame particular Christians, but with the wider purpose of slandering Christianity itself. This degrading movement gathered momentum with each meeting, and any church that refused to participate was noted carefully. In this way, one by one, China's churches were being assimilated into the Three Self program, which in reality stood for "control by the State, financial dependence on the State, and propagation in line with the ideology of the State."[4]

After weakening much of the church's infrastructure, it was time to focus on her most popular leader. Watchman was probably not astonished on November 30 to read an article in *Tien Feng* entitled, "A Revelation of the Secret Organization and Dark Doings of the Little Flock Church." What might have surprised him was that it was written by a member of one of his own congregations. The article was as absurd as its author:

"I am a believer who from the outset has belonged to the Little Flock church in Nanking and who regarded it as the purest of assemblies until I was indoctrinated regarding the Three Self Reform Movement, when I saw plainly what a vile place it is. I have long been deceived, but today I stand on the ground of love of country and love of religion, and with emotions of unqualified wrath I expose its professed 'spirituality.' In order to conceal the true antirevolutionary nature of this movement, those in responsibility at the church persistently and emphatically affirm that it is a 'local church.' As a matter of fact we have been utterly misled. From its very inception it has been subject to the Shanghai assembly and

is strictly controlled by Watchman Nee. It is an organized system of nationwide and occult character.
Watchman Nee has an involved, secret system for
controlling 470 churches all over the country, with
Shanghai as his administrative base. The dark, mys-
terious control Watchman Nee exercises over the
churches goes quite beyond the sphere of religion.
To facilitate his totalitarian control, he disseminates
antirevolutionary poison and dominates the thought
of church members. He shamelessly terms himself
'an apostle of God!' " [5]

After reading the article, Ruth Lee came to
Watchman and even though she could predict what his
response would be, she asked, "What will you do to
defend yourself against these ridiculous accusations?"

"You know better than most, dear friend, how
God has dealt with me in the past," he answered.
"After I was excommunicated from the fellowship in
Foochow as a young man, a great revival followed in
that area. Then the Lord used a serious illness to help
me choose to devote my life to the local church
instead of becoming a popular evangelist. Then during the Japanese war, He forced me through my own
friends to withdraw from the ministry for a season,
only to bring me back with greater energy and understanding. And now this," he said, his brow furrowed
but his eyes as bright as ever. "Why should this experience be different from all the others? No, dear
Ruth, I will not retaliate. This has all the signs of
God at work again in my life. He has more to teach

me and I will not refuse the gift. Besides, there is always some element of truth in every criticism." With that, he excused himself and went to be alone so that he could pray before the upcoming accusation meeting to be held in his own church.

Before that meeting would be staged, there was still much ministry to be done. Watchman and his coworkers began to work around the clock to prepare biblical materials for the believers who would be left behind. The workers averaged two hours of sleep a night as Watchman dictated new lessons to Ruth Lee and her assistants. He would pace back and forth, expounding God's Word into the early hours of the morning. With little voice left, he would then collapse into bed for a brief nap before rising to take up the task again. This continued until the inevitable footsteps of soldiers sounded in his street and he responded to the loud rap at his door. Watchman embraced Charity, said good-bye to her, and shouted to his friends, "Tell them in Hong Kong to dissociate all secular business enterprise from the church!"

He was arrested by officers of the Department of Public Safety on April 10, 1952, and charged as a lawless capitalist. He was fifty years old and would never know another moment of human freedom.

sixteen

Watchman didn't complain about the rats in his cell, the miserable food, the sleep deprivation, or the rest of the hardships of prison life. But he did miss his beloved Bible. It was the first thing the guards took from him. Because he was not allowed to communicate with anyone in the outside world, few specifics are known about the suffering he endured for the next twenty years. Even if he had been given permission to write of his condition, he would never have revealed his suffering. And so Angus Kinnear writes in *Against the Tide,*

> *Fierce attempts were made to re-educate him into acquiescence in the national neurosis; a supine renunciation of all freedom of thought. We have ample documentation of the thought-reform methods then in use: the long*

hours of questioning by relays of interroga-
tors, the political lectures, the vigilant
scrutiny of relentless warders, the occupa-
tion of his cell by convinced and converted
'fellow students,' and the strident speak-
bitterness of the group struggle meetings.
That no change of heart took place and no
confession worth using emerged speaks
volumes for the keeping power of God.[1]

By the time the accusation meeting was scheduled, the authorities had created an indictment 2,296
pages in length. The charges ranged from imperialist intrigue and espionage to counterrevolutionary
activities hostile to government policy, gross im-
morality, and financial irregularities. The Communists did all they could to stir the members of the
church into an angry denunciation of their pastor as
an enemy of the people. But the few statements they
were able to solicit were too preposterous for serious consideration.

When Ruth Lee, Peace Wang, and Dr. C. H. Yu
were summoned before the congregation, they boldly
refused to make any kind of accusation. They were
rewarded by being arrested the very next day, along
with several others. The following week saw at least
thirty leaders in the Shanghai church taken into cus-
tody. In fact, a general sweep of Little Flock churches
throughout China was ordered, and in this way as
many as two thousand key believers were incarcerated,

disappearing from their families and friends, often never to be seen again.

In the meantime, Watchman stood before his government-appointed accusers for twelve long days, listening to page after page of the bogus indictment being read to him. The hours passed, but he remained silent as his Lord who went before him had done, as "the sheep before his shearer is dumb." Finally the vice-mayor of Shanghai stood and addressed the church audience of more than twenty-five hundred:

"The opposition of Nee and his gang to the Three Self movement is not a matter of religious principle," he bellowed to the standing-room-only crowd. "Religion is religion and faith is faith; they must not be mixed up with a person's private counterrevolutionary ideas and used as a cover behind which to spread the poison of hatred toward country and people. Every Christian should enter positively into the struggle to expose these arrested men's crimes."

He looked cunningly around the congregation and added, "We still have serious questions about a number of others also, but for the present we let them alone to see if they will repent and show a new attitude. You members of the Little Flock churches should not be afraid of washing your dirty linen in public but should vigorously seek out and expose all offenders. This struggle has just begun. We will not draw back until we have completed it victoriously and rooted out every counterrevolutionary hidden within the Little Flock."[2]

After the grueling ordeal, Watchman was taken back to his prison cell. But his public humiliation was far from finished. The very next day, the *Liberation Daily,* Shanghai's largest newspaper, published an editorial cartoon with the caption "Render Up" beneath it. It pictured a two-story house, with people on the upper floor pressing toward a masked burglar sitting on a stepladder demanding that they empty their possessions into a large funnel labeled "Render Unto God the Things That Are God's." All kinds of gifts were pouring down the funnel, including a coolie's shirt and the coat that he took off his own weeping child. On the floor below was a bin labeled, "For the Work of Counterrevolution." At the mouth of the receptacle a caricature of Watchman Nee was drawn, greedily grasping at the flow of gold, jewelry, watches, and money as a prostitute sat on his lap.

Immediately after the media onslaught, church leaders throughout the region were ordered to take special measures to inform Christians everywhere of "the crimes of Watchman Nee." To advance the scandal, the February issue of *Tien Feng* ran an eleven-page article exposing Pastor Nee's vices, entitled "Drive the Cruel Wolves Out of the Church." Using pseudoreligious doublespeak, its author concluded, "Watchman Nee and his gang have been destructive of our economic reconstruction, dangerous to the people's livelihood and social order, and a threat to national safety. Their presence within the

Christian church has been a dishonor to the holy name of the Lord, a blot on the church's reputation, and a corruption of gospel truth. They are very clever and devious and like to talk about holiness. Their own actions, however, are far from holy, and the life of Watchman Nee himself is too adulterous to repeat.

"Brothers and sisters, we are very happy that this gang can never again disturb and harm our beloved church, and so we may now unite freely in mutual love. Fellow Christians, let us celebrate our common victory. It is only by exposing and expelling such wolves that we can purify the church so that it may glorify the Lord."[3]

There followed a systematic program for "brainwashing" members of the Little Flock churches all over China. Believers were given the opportunity to publicly confess their wrongdoing and join the Three Self movement. Many who refused were arrested and seemingly dropped from existence. All prayer meetings, Bible studies, and other unauthorized Christian activities in private homes were declared illegal and severely enforced. Itinerant preachers were declared to be outlaws and were rigorously sought by the police. It was only a little while later that the "reorientation" of Watchman's congregation in Shanghai was pronounced complete. Its official entry into the Three Self movement followed quickly. The government could now claim that "the whole Protestant church in China is united under a single authority."[4]

In the meantime, Charity's name made the "wanted"

list. But ill from stress and on the verge of losing her eyesight from hypertension, she was admitted to a hospital and placed under strict medical care and police surveillance. As soon as they deemed her recovered enough to travel, she was arrested and taken to prison. Because her husband had no means of communication, he did not know of her suffering.

Watchman settled in for the mind-breaking grind of prison life. His day was divided into eight hours of harsh labor, eight hours of "re-education," and eight hours of dark loneliness in his cell. He froze in the winter and experienced insufferable heat in the summer—always vigilant to look for things that crawled to supplement his diet. After several years of near-starvation, his body was weak and skeletal. But his mind remained sharp and his spirit indomitable.

He refused to denounce any of his coworkers (just as Ruth Lee and Peace Wang remained incarcerated because they would not lie about him) and held fast to his faith and integrity under severe pressure. While the loudspeakers blasted propaganda throughout the drab and grisly prison, he recited Scripture aloud and kept his mind stayed on the peace of Christ. More than one prisoner released from the First Place of Detention reported that they would go to sleep at night listening to a sweet baritone voice singing self-composed Scripture songs from behind Watchman's cell door.

But the old British dungeon wasn't the only place God was working. Although Chairman Mao's "Great Leap Forward" included the closing of all evangelical churches and the forced suppression of biblical Christianity, irrepressible faith continued to break out in little pockets all over China. A revival started up among students, largely fueled by Watchman Nee's writings. Like their imprisoned hero, these courageous young men and women committed themselves to memorize entire chapters and books of the New Testament—in case they might one day be stripped of their Bibles. *Tien Feng* reported that the police were discovering the "wicked activities" of counterrevolutionaries everywhere they went, like faith-healing and the casting out of demons. That same year, Watchman's book, *The Normal Christian Life,* was published in Bombay, India, and a new work began there.

Originally sentenced to fifteen years for crimes against the government, Watchman frequently heard the ancient public address system announce: "If you have a five-year or a seven-year sentence, and if when your term is up we are not satisfied that you have changed, you will be given a further five or seven years." Watchman's fifteen years were up in April 1967. Charity had been released in poor health and awaited his return to their home in Shanghai. Christians throughout the world were praying for his freedom, but no word came.

Finally a report reached the Little Flock church in Hong Kong that the People's Republic had been offered a large ransom from believers in the West as well as in Asia. The account stated that the Chinese government was willing to allow both Watchman and Charity to "defect to the West" upon payment. But no sooner had the church begun to hope again than a statement was released saying that the deal was off. Those who knew Pastor Nee best were not surprised. He who fathomed the Scriptures better than any of them would not have forgotten the description of the imprisoned believers in Hebrews chapter eleven: "Others were tortured and refused to be released, so that they might gain a better resurrection." Watchman was seeking a better resurrection and wouldn't deny whatever suffering God had planned for him.

God was not through with Watchman's ministry in the prison. He had learned to say with the apostle Paul, "Pray also for me, that whenever I open my mouth, words may be given me so that I will fearlessly make known the mystery of the gospel, for which I am an ambassador in chains. Pray that I may declare it fearlessly, as I should." With great boldness, he evangelized every person within earshot of his cell block.

In May 1968, a Chinese refugee seeking political asylum in a Western capital came out with an intriguing story. He related how he had been a prison guard at the First Place of Detention in Shanghai. There he had experienced the hatred of the worst of China's criminal element, and the last person he expected to meet in that wretched place was the Son of God. But through the steady witness of a longtime prisoner, a certain "To-sheng Nee," he had accepted Jesus Christ as Lord and Savior, and his life was changed forever. It is obvious that Watchman never viewed his imprisonment as a *punishment* for preaching the gospel but rather as a *platform* for the same.

Word reached Watchman that Charity was dead. He knew that she had been holding on by hoping that after he served a full twenty years in prison, the authorities might still release him. But just a few months short of that date, she lost her footing while standing on a stool in the little home she was preparing for his return. The broken ribs and internal injuries were too much for her to survive. Her husband took the news hard.

On April 12, 1972, he completed his twentieth year in chains, suffering from a painful heart condition, and still his captors would not give him freedom. But they did allow him a limited form of communication by this time, although he was forbidden to mention the name of God in any letters. On April 22, he wrote a letter to his sister:

Elder Sister,

I have received your letter of April 7, and learn from it that you have not had my acknowledgment of the things you sent me. Everything you name has in fact reached me and I am most grateful to you. You know the chronic condition I have is always with me. The attacks of course are distressing, but in the intervals it is not so difficult. Still, I

maintain my own joy, so please do not
worry. And I hope you also take care of
yourself, and that joy fills your heart.

Wishing you well,
Shu-tsu

These are the last words anyone outside the
Shanghai prison ever heard from Watchman Nee, and
they are noteworthy for two reasons: First, this lovely
yet physically broken man, almost sixty-nine years of
age, signed his last letter with his childhood name,
"Shu-tsu." To the very end, he remained common,
with a childlike faith. And secondly, although he was
prohibited from mentioning God's name, the Spirit of
Christ fills this final communiqué. Just as Jesus had
talked more about His "cup of joy" being filled the
closer He came to the cross, so His bondslave, Shu-tsu,
maintained His joy as death approached.

On June 1, Watchman entered into eternal joy
and rejoined Charity. What he had preached so passionately to others was now completely realized in
his death:

"Nothing hurts so much," he once said, "as dis-
satisfaction with our circumstances. We all start from
rest, but there is another rest which we discover
when we learn from Jesus how to say, 'I thank you,
Father, for it seemed good to Thee.' God knows what
He is doing and there is nothing accidental in the life
of the believer. Nothing but good can come to those
who are wholly His."

"To what are we committed? Not to Christian work, but to the will of God, to be and to do whatever He pleases. The path of every Christian has been already marked out by God. If at the close of a life we can say with Paul, 'I have finished my course,' then we are blessed indeed. The Old Testament saints served their own generation and passed on. Men go, but the Lord remains. God Himself takes away His workers, but He gives others. Our work suffers, but never His. He is still God."[5]

"Precious in the sight of the Lord is the death of his saints" (Psalm 116:15).

epilogue

Lai Peng is a twenty-two-year-old Chinese evangelist. Recently, at a meeting of one of China's "house churches" (a weekly prayer meeting not sanctioned by the government), he and four other evangelists were seized by agents of the Public Security Bureau (China's version of the KGB). The police dragged Lai Peng and his young Christian friends in front of the entire congregation and severely beat them. The security officers then handed the heavy clubs to various members of the church and ordered them to abuse the preachers, on pain of being thrashed themselves.

Pastor Lai was so badly injured that the authorities feared he would die in their presence, leaving them in an embarrassing situation. Therefore they released him and pushed him down the street away from the scene of his beating. The pitiful preacher hobbled for several miles, eventually succumbing to his injuries. He collapsed and died on the road to his home.

Tom Strode reports for the Ethics and Religious Liberty Commission that Chinese believers included the following reports in their interviews with the Freedom House team:

- The normal sentence for illegal church activities is three years of "re-education through labor" in a prison camp. Usually this sentence is given on the third offense for church members, often on the first offense for church leaders and normally for preachers found outside their home area.
- Eighty-five underground Christians were arrested in Henan Province in May.
- About 40 percent of inmates in Henan labor camps are imprisoned for house-church activities.
- In December in Hebei Province, several underground church members were detained at a train station for carrying imported Bibles and suffered crippling beatings from the security police. They still are unable to walk without aid.
- Joseph Zhongliang, the underground Catholic bishop of Shanghai, is under virtual house arrest with police surveillance.

In effect, he is prevented from meeting with foreigners.[1]

The respected group Amnesty International released a report this year that relates the macabre stories of Chinese Christian women being hung by their thumbs from wires, beaten with heavy rods, and shocked with electric probes. Such persecution and oppression of believers is commonplace in China today.

Forbes magazine calls it "one of the most under-reported stories in the world today." The Hudson Institute's Michael Horowitz calls it "eerily parallel" to the Jewish situation in Europe several decades ago. And recent testimony before Congress called it "a rising tide of terrorism and human rights abuses."

Twenty-six years after Watchman Nee's ignominious death for the cause of Christ, the strategy to silence China's finest Christian leaders is still in place. Nineteen church leaders were arrested in early August in An Hui Province in the middle of their Bible-training conference. Many of them have been in and out of prison since 1983 and have horrific tales of torture to show for their faithfulness.

According to the China Christian Council, the Communist government's watchdog group for evangelical "disruption," the "crimes" of these pastors are usually always twofold: They preach on the Second Coming of Christ (still an illegal activity in China), and they refuse to join the Three Self movement (to come under governmental control). As always, China says it doesn't seek to eradicate religion but rather to control it.

An overt policy of exterminating Christians would cause worldwide outrage. Ever since the normalization of relations with the United States, China has announced their religious policy as one of "freedom within limits." What this means to Chinese believers is that all pastoral ministry, Bible studies, training activities, church planting, training activities, and overseas Christian contacts can only take place within the officially recognized church structures and under the direct supervision of the Communist Party. Activities outside this system are declared illegal, with Christians subject to harassment, detention, fines, arrest, and imprisonment. Beatings, torture, and even death are not unusual while under arrest.

Even if the Chinese Christians aren't physically abused by the authorities as Watchman Nee was and the martyrs who followed him have been, they are persecuted on perhaps an even deeper level—systematic discrimination against believers in a social context. Because their beliefs are considered superstitious and unscientific, Christians are usually denied good jobs or educational opportunities. Party members are forbidden to believe in religion. Government officials view Christianity as a genuine threat to their authority.

In fact, the persecution of Christians in China today is probably more brutal than it was at the time of Watchman Nee's arrest—and the reason for that is obvious to some. The escalating oppression is "absolutely tied to the collapse of the Soviet Empire," said Nina Shea, director of the Puebla Program. The Communist Party is "terrified of Christian beliefs," Shea reported. "They are fearful of the notion of individual liberty and a transcendent God. They observed the role of the churches in the fall of Communism in Eastern Europe and now see the churches on their own borders as a threat. If China were to become Christian, the history of the twenty-first century would be totally different than if it remained atheistic."

According to the *Mindszenty Report,* a February 1996 internal Communist Party document estimated that more Chinese have joined Christian groups in recent years than the party. While today there are approximately fifty-three million party members, there are probably twice that number of believers. No wonder Christians are facing the harshest persecution of their faiths since the cultural revolution of the 1960s.

Watchman Nee was arrested forty-six years ago. The Chinese government has had a half-century to cripple the cause of Christianity and thwart its growth. But the faith has not even been checked in China. "On the contrary," says Nina Shea, "the government's campaign has produced the greatest period of Christian growth in China's history."[1]

Representatives of the Freedom House claim that churches report a three- to fourfold increase in membership since 1990 and a more than tenfold increase since 1980. Estimates of the total number of Christians in China today range from 60 to 100 million. One church last year baptized 1,450 believers in a single day. One small province baptized 60,000 in less than a year.

"Ironically," says Paul Marshall, author of *Their Blood Cries Out,* "the very campaign to eradicate the underground churches by the government may be spurring their growth. Underground leaders say the commitment required to practice one's faith in China leads to a strong, disciplined, and growing church."

One of Pastor Nee's most often quoted Bible verses was 2 Timothy 3:12: "Everyone who wants to live a godly life in Christ Jesus will be persecuted." He accepted oppression as his destiny, buying up the opportunities to prove God's strength through his own personal weakness. In fact, near the end of his life, Watchman wrote some advice to his friends that especially applies to the persecuted believers in China today:

"Love not the world, neither the things that are in the world." You have an anointing from the Holy One: live by it! Give yourself to God; live for Him wholly and utterly; see to it that, where you personally are concerned, the things of this world are scored off Satan's books and transferred to God's account. For "the world and its desires pass away, but the man who does the will of God lives forever."

185

But just because "the Spirit of glory and of God rests on you" when you "are insulted because of the name of Christ" (1 Peter 4:14), that doesn't mean that believers today should sit silently while their brothers and sisters are unjustly persecuted in other parts of the world. More Christians have been martyred for their faith in this century alone than in the previous nineteen centuries combined.

The singular reason that the people of Israel were finally released from their bondage in Egypt was because one man obeyed God's call to speak out. Moses broke the silence. Just as an otherwise obscure king named Lemuel spoke up in his day, so his words still speak to our generation today:

"SPEAK UP FOR THOSE WHO
CANNOT SPEAK FOR THEMSELVES,
FOR THE RIGHTS OF ALL
WHO ARE DESTITUTE."
(Proverbs 31:8)

Endnotes

Chapter One
1. Kinnear, Angus I. *Against the Tide: The Story of Watchman Nee.* Christian Literature Crusade. Fort Washington, Pennsylvania: 1973, p. 23. Copyright © 1973 by Angus I. Kinnear. Used by permission of Kingsway Publications, Eastbourne, UK.
2. Lee, Witness. *Watchman Nee: A Seer of the Divine Revelation in the Present Age.* Living Stream Ministry. Anaheim, California: 1991, p. 12. Copyright © 1991 by Living Stream Ministry. Used by permission.

Chapter Two
1. Kinnear, p. 32
2. Kinnear, p. 33
3. Lee, p. 13
4. Lee, p. 12
5. Lee, p. 14

Chapter Three
1. Lee, p. 20
2. Lee, p. 64

Chapter Four
1. Lee, p. 45
2. Kinnear, p. 40
3. Kinnear, p. 41

4. Lee, p. 25

5. Nee, Watchman. *Love Not the World*. Tyndale HousePublishers, Inc. Wheaton, Illinois: 1978, p. 32. Copyright © 1968 by Angus I. Kinnear. Used by permission of Kingsway Publications, Eastbourne, UK.

6. Lee, p. 37

7. Lee, p. 40

8. Lee, p. 42

9. Lee, p. 43

10. Lee, p. 43

Chapter Five

1. Kinnear, p. 45

2. Kinnear, p. 53

3. Lee, p. 33

4. Lee, p. 50

5. Lee, p. 58

Chapter Six

1. Kinnear, p. 66

2. Kinnear, p. 69

3. Kinnear, p. 71

4. Lee, p. 92

5. Lee, p. 91

Chapter Seven

1. Kinnear, p. 71

2. Kinnear, pp. 74-75

3. Lee, p. 141

4. Kinnear, p. 81

5. Kinnear, p. 81

6. Lee, p. 19

Chapter Eight

1. Kinnear, p. 94

2. Kinnear, p. 86

3. Kinnear, p. 87

4. Lee, p. 232

Chapter Nine
1. Kinnear, p. 92
2. Kinnear, p. 92

Chapter Ten
1. Certain statements or observations made by Watchman Nee in this conversation have been adapted and excerpted from Chapter 12, "How to Lead People to Christ," in Nee, *The Good Confession* (New York: Christian Fellowship Publishers, 1973), pp. 75-77. Used by permission of the Publishers.

Chapter Eleven
1. Kinnear, p. 99
2. Kinnear, p. 101
3. Kinnear, p. 101
4. Lee, p. 175
5. Kinnear, p. 107
6. A few of the statements and observations made by Watchman Nee, as found in the last half of the discussion presented here among the Shanghai church elders, have been adapted and excerpted from Chapter 10, "The Elimination of Distinctions," in Nee, *The Good Confession* (New York: Christian Fellowship Publishers, 1973), pp. 36, 39-40. Used by permission of the Publishers.
7. Kinnear, p. 103

Chapter Twelve
1. Lee, p. 267-269
2. Kinnear, p. 111
3. Kinnear, pp. 111-112

Chapter Thirteen
1. Kinnear, p. 116
2. Certain statements and observations made by Watchman Nee in his teaching on prayer here to his people have been adapted and excerpted from Chapter 6, "Prayer," in Nee, *A Living Sacrifice,*

(New York: Christian Fellowship Publishers, 1972), pp. 85, 87-89.
Used by permission of the Publishers

3. Kinnear, p. 117
4. Kinnear, p. 118
5. Lee, p. 149

Chapter Fourteen
1. Kinnear, p. 121
2. Kinnear, p. 123
3. Kinnear, p. 135
4. Kinnear, p. 135

Chapter Fifteen
1. Kinnear, p. 139
2. Kinnear, p. 145
3. Kinnear, p. 146
4. Kinnear, p. 152
5. Kinnear, p. 153

Chapter Sixteen
1. Kinnear, p. 155
2. Kinnear, p. 163
3. Kinnear, p. 165
4. Kinnear, p. 167
5. Kinnear, p. 174

Epilogue
1. Strode, Tom. "China Intensifies Persecution." A report from *The Ethics and Religious Liberty Commission of the Southern Baptist Convention,* 1997.

Bibliography

Nee, Watchman. *Love Not the World*. Tyndale House Publishers, Inc. Wheaton, Illinois: 1978.

Nee, Watchman. *The Good Confession*. Christian Fellowship Publishers, Inc. New York: 1973.

Nee, Watchman. *Spiritual Reality or Obsession*. Christian Fellowship Publishers, Inc. New York: 1970.

Nee, Watchman. *Sit, Walk, Stand*. Christian Fellowship Publishers, Inc. New York: 1971.

Nee, Watchman. *The Normal Christian Life*. Christian Fellowship Publishers, Inc. New York: 1972.

Nee, Watchman. *A Living Sacrifice*. Christian Fellowship Publishers, Inc. New York: 1972.

Lee, Witness. *Watchman Nee: A Seer of the Divine Revelation in the Present Age*. Living Stream Ministry. Anaheim, California: 1991.

Kinnear, Angus I. *Against the Tide: The Story of Watchman Nee*. Christian Literature Crusade. Fort Washington, Pennsylvania: 1973.

Ellis, Elisabeth Gaynor and Esler, Anthony. *World History: Connections to Today*. Prentice-Hall, Inc. Needham, Massachusetts: 1997.

Strode, Tom. "China Intensifies Persecution." A report from *The Ethics and Religious Liberty Commission of the Southern Baptist Convention*, 1997.

The Mindszenty Report. Cardinal Mindszenty Foundation. April, 1997.

Snyder, Steven L. "When Silence Is Not Golden." *WEF Religious Liberty Commission*. October 8, 1997.

Charen, Mona. "Suffering for the Faith." *The Washington Times*. October 3, 1996.

HEROES OF THE FAITH

This exciting biographical series explores the lives of famous Christian men and women throughout the ages. These trade paper books will inspire encourage you to follow the example of these "Heroes of the Faith" made Christ the center of their existence. 208 pages each. Only $3.97 ea

Gladys Aylward, Missionary to China
Sam Wellman

Brother Andrew, God's Undercover Agent
Alan Millwright

Corrie ten Boom, Heroine of Haarlem
Sam Wellman

*William and Catherine Booth,
Founders of the Salvation Army*
Helen Hosier

*John Bunyan,
Author of* The Pilgrim's Progress
Sam Wellman

William Carey, Father of Missions
Sam Wellman

Amy Carmichael, Abandoned to God
Sam Wellman

Fanny Crosby, the Hymn Writer
Bernard Ruffin

Frederick Douglass, Abolitionist and Reformer
Rachael Phillips

Jonathan Edwards, The Great Awakener
Helen Hosier

Jim Elliot, Missionary to Ecuador
Susan Miller

Charles Finney, The Great Revivalist
Bonnie Harvey

Billy Graham, the Great Evangelist
Sam Wellman

Eric Liddell, Olympian and Missionary
Ellen Caughey

C.S. Lewis, Author of Mere Christianity
Sam Wellman

Martin Luther, the Great Reformer
Dan Harmon

George Müller, Man of Faith
Bonnie Harvey

David Livingstone, Missionary and Explo
Sam Wellman

*George Washington Carver,
Inventor and Naturalist*
Sam Wellman

D.L. Moody, the American Evangelist
Bonnie Harvey

Samuel Morris, the Apostle of Simple Fa
W. Terry Whalin

Mother Teresa, Missionary of Charity
Sam Wellman

Watchman Nee, Man of Suffering
Bob Laurent

John Newton, Author of "Amazing Grac
Anne Sandberg

Florence Nightingale, Lady with the Lan
Sam Wellman

Mary Slessor, Queen of Calabar
Sam Wellman

Charles Spurgeon, the Great Orator
Dan Harmon

Hudson Taylor, Founder, China Inland Mis
Vance Christie

Sojourner Truth, American Abolitionis
W. Terry Whalin

John Wesley, the Great Methodist
Sam Wellman

Available wherever books are sold.
Or order from:
Barbour Publishing, Inc.
P.O. Box 719
Uhrichsville, Ohio 44683
http://www.barbourbooks.com

If you order by mail, add $2.00 to your order for shipping.
Prices subject to change without notice.